You Must Relax
discusses the following important subjects
among many others:

Tension
Anxiety
Fears and Success
Overactive Nerves
Tranquilizers
How to Relax Lying Down
How to Relax While Active
Common Nervous Disorders
The Quest for Sleep
How to Sleep Well
Indigestion and Colitis
What Causes High Blood Pressure
How to Save Your Heart

Dr. Edmund Jacobson first presented lectures
on the scientific method of "relaxation" at
Harvard University in 1908. He continues his
research work in this vital field as Director
of the Laboratory for Clinical Physiology,
Chicago.

McGRAW-HILL PAPERBACKS
GUIDES, HOBBIES AND PERSONAL DEVELOPMENT BOOKS

Dr. Dorothy W. Baruch, How to Live With Your Teenager	$1.95
James F. Bender, How To Talk Well	1.95
H. J. Bernhard, D. A. Bennett, and M. S. Rice, New Handbook of the Heavens	2.25
Pilaff Bey, Venus in the Kitchen	1.75
Miriam Bredow, Handbook for the Medical Secretary	2.65
P. T. Brockwell, Jr., How to Repair Household Appliances	2.25
Fred Brown and Rudolph T. Kempton, Sex Questions and Answers	1.95
Laurence E. Burton, Weekend Painter	2.45
Robert Calvert, Jr. and John E. Steele, Planning Your Career	1.95
J. Ralph Dalzell, Remodeling Guide for Home Interiors	2.45
Ruth Fedder, A Girl Grows Up	1.95
John Henderson, M.D., Emergency Medical Guide	2.95
Edmund Jacobson, You Must Relax	2.45
Kenneth S. Keyes, Jr., How to Develop Your Thinking Ability	2.15
Donald A. and Eleanor C. Laird, Techniques for Efficient Remembering	1.75
Paul J. Leedy, Improve Your Reading	2.85
Louis A. Leslie and Kenneth B. Coffin, Handbook for the Legal Secretary	2.95
Beth McLean and Jeanne Paris, The Young Woman in Business	2.35
William Marcus and Alex Levy, Practical Radio Servicing	3.95
Lucy G. Mayo, Communications Handbook for Secretaries	3.95
Richard M. Pearl, How to Know the Minerals and Rocks	1.45
Herbert Pollack and Arthur D. Morse, How to Reduce Surely and Safely	1.45
Joseph Shoenfelt, Designing and Making Handwrought Jewelry	1.95
Robert L. Shurter, Effective Letters in Business	1.95
Robert L. Shurter, Handy Grammar Reference	1.25
Evelyn S. Stead and Gloria K. Warren, Low-fat Cookery	1.95
Sidney Sulkin, Complete Planning for College	3.95
J. Douglas Wilson, Practical House Carpentry	2.95
Harold P. Zelko, Successful Conference and Discussion Techniques	2.75

Sports and Games

Richard Kraus, The Family Book of Games	$1.75
Maribel Y. Vinson, Primer of Figure Skating	2.45

Prices subject to change without notice.

You Must Relax
Edmund Jacobson, M.D.

4th edition, revised and enlarged

McGRAW-HILL BOOK COMPANY, INC.
New York   Toronto   London

YOU MUST RELAX

Published by the McGraw-Hill Book Company, Inc.,
by arrangement with the University of Chicago Press

To My Mother

Preface

This is a tense world, as many of us well know. We talk about "tension" and we read about it. It is discussed in newspaper articles, in magazines and in books. Evidently, there is growing popular realization of something excessive in our way of living which can lead to disorder and malady. There is search for remedy. Today doctors tell us to "relax".

This was not always so. When the famous physician who attended President Wilson wrote a book about rest, the word "relaxation" did not even appear in the index. People then did not discuss tension. The characters in movies written in that epoch did not tell each other to "relax" as they do nowadays, for the word had not yet sunk into the popular mores. I know, because ten years previously I had begun to develop the principles and the scientific study of tension and relaxation as we now know them.

I felt the burden of responsibility deeply. On the one hand I must test each advance in the field objectively, avoiding any enthusiasm which could cloud my judgment. Yet in my cold analysis as a scientist, I must not close my eyes to any light which could guide mankind.

My investigations were begun in the laboratory at Harvard University in 1908. Later I carried them further at Cornell and at the University of Chicago until 1936. Since then they have been conducted in a laboratory to which I have devoted my private means and my time, the Laboratory for Clinical Physiology in Chicago. The results of these investigations afforded practical measures for improving the nervous status of human beings. These practical measures have been tested and have been developed further over the years in my associated clinics.

My studies led to definite understanding of what tension really is, namely, the effort which is manifested in shortening of muscle fibers. Physiologists know this as muscle tension and have studied it in animals for over a century. I was attempting to begin where they left off in order to turn some of the vast basic knowledge which they had accumulated toward the benefit of man.

As I went along, I wrote up some of the results and they appeared in scientific journals. Believing that the universal trend toward overactive minds and bodies could result in various ills, I wrote a book in 1929 called *Progressive Relaxation*. It was addressed to doctors and other scientists. Some said that it was very technical. Accordingly, the suggestion was made that I write in simpler form for laymen. I did so under the title *You Must Relax*. Since then many physicians have prescribed it as reading matter for their patients.

My path led through many difficulties. At first I had to contend with the fact that doctors and laymen alike were prone to think of amusement, recreation or hobbies at the mention of the word "relax".

Therefore I had to choose between (1) inventing a new word to mean neuromuscular relaxation and (2) trying to lead the public to use a word already familiar to them in the sense of recreation or hobby but diverted to mean neuromuscular relaxation. I chose the latter course. As the years have gone by, I have not regretted the decision. To an appreciable extent, the public has "caught on", and today the word "relax" has become part and parcel of daily speech in the sense of "let go" or "take it easy".

High nervous tension is prevalent in America today, leading to tension disorders of various types which will be discussed in this volume in an elementary manner.

What we know about the nervous system and the mind, what we know from investigation by electrical methods can be synthesized in one very important principle: relaxation is the direct negative of nervous excitement. It is the absence of nerve-muscle impulse. More simply said, *to be relaxed is the direct physiological opposite of being excited or disturbed.*

Is this obvious? I hope so, for I have worked hard over the years to make it become so. If it is even beginning to become incorporated into the thinking of the medical student, I am very glad. But let him draw the conclusions: nervous disturbance is at the same time mental disturbance. Neurosis and psychoneurosis are at the same time physiological disturbance; for they are forms of tension disorder. Thus whatever the psychiatrist accomplishes by his therapy, this accomplishment necessarily must consist in the diminution of neuromuscular excitability. And the success of any method used by the psychiatrist must be eventually in terms of the habitual relaxation which he has accomplished in and for his patient.

Tension is an objective manifestation of what all of us know in ourselves as effort. The same word is used not only for the effort which is in our every act, but also for an excess thereof. Thus, in one context, "tension" may mean reasonable effort, in another, excessive effort. Once this matter is clarified, we can judge from the context whether the word "tension" is to be interpreted as meaning necessary effort or excessive effort.

In the newly added chapters I have tried to show more clearly how our efforts to achieve the smaller and the greater forms of success for which all of us strive can lead to tension disorders when these efforts become greater than our bodies can bear. But the aim of this volume is to preserve and to develop what is best in our efforts through a better internal organization. By learning to save ourselves physiologically we can take steps to prevent tension disorders.

Tension disorders include various common nervous disorders, including states of fear and anxiety, and they are often involved also in conditions known as peptic ulcer, nervous indigestion, spastic colon, high blood pressure, and coronary heart attacks. These conditions are discussed in the new chapters.

As will be set forth, the evidence indicates that our susceptibility to these conditions varies with our heredity as well as with the environment, including the pressures to which we are exposed. Taking into account all that is known today about the incidence of coronary heart disease, we cannot rule out the influence of heredity, for in the male the lining of the coronary vessels is much thicker at birth than in the female, in whom the incidence is much less. We do not yet know enough about the causes of fat deposit in this lining to say whether a diet rich in cholesterol really adds to the incidence of coronary disease. We must wait for further evidence. But we do have sufficient evidence, I believe, to permit us to make a general statement on the nature of "heart attacks".

This condition, we can now say, generally is a complication of coronary arteriosclerosis plus tension. The greater the tension or the more advanced the sclerosis, the more likely the complication. We do not know all the causes of sclerosis, but evidence will be presented that tension favors its development.

This book, then, is written to teach people how to conserve their energies, thereby to avoid undue tension, yet ever striving for the success which seems to them good. Its purpose is to encourage them to take the advantage of the "built-in tranquilizer" which exists ready for use in every one of us. Why use sedatives and tranquilizing drugs with their many side-effects, asks my lifelong friend, Oscar G. Mayer—who originated the expression quoted —when nature has provided a built-in device free from all such defects?

To help in this direction of preventive medicine but also to train doctors and educators in respective fields of medicine and of education, there has recently been formed the Foundation for Scientific Relaxation. It is incorporated not for profit. Thus it is a philanthropy which, in the opinion of its staff of businessmen, doctors and other scientists, can do much for the public welfare.

I realize that a popular book on fatigue and nervous ills might prompt many to try to use it for self-healing when what they really need is instruction in the method by a physician, or some other form of medical attention. It is our hope through the Foundation eventually to have physicians trained in the field available to the public in various sections of the country.

EDMUND JACOBSON, M.D.

Laboratory for Clinical Physiology, Chicago

Acknowledgments

For encouragement and advice I am indebted to the late Dr. Anton J. Carlson, until 1936 my senior officer at the University of Chicago; and for support and technical aid as long as I needed it to the Bell Telephone Laboratories, especially to Dr. Mervin J. Kelley, the President.

Contents

YOU MUST RELAX

1

Modern Living

For a long time living at high tension has been the order of the day. As far back as 1880, George Miller Beard called attention to the prevalence of nervousness in this country. Since then, with the advent of the express train, the automobile and the plane, the telephone, the radio and the television, it is well known that the pace of life has generally increased. At the same time opportunity and competition have developed not alone in business but also in the social, professional and educational worlds, so that almost every individual in modern life is obliged to meet demands on his nervous energy which would not have been made many years ago.

The career of the average businessman is a familiar example of high-tension living. As a rule he engages almost throughout the day in a series of activities involving considerable nerve tension. If successful, he is stimulated to attempts at greater and better achievement; if in difficulty, he is likely to spare no effort to reach security. Fatigue sometimes remains unnoticed until he finds himself almost exhausted mentally. Unfortunately, when he

leaves his place of business for the day his cares generally
go with him. Tensions which have been present during the
preceding hours are likely to continue in the background
of his evening occupations. In many instances his recrea-
tions fail to bring adequate refreshment. As I shall try to
show later, he fails to relax.

Social affairs in modern life often prove no less wearing.
The hostess at a dinner party or reception may spend
many trying hours arranging details not apparent to the
casual observer, and she frequently is not at ease until the
entire event lies in the past. Attendance at cocktail parties
and other functions, often carried far into the night, may
produce more fatigue than an equal number of hours of
accustomed work. This is especially likely if the gaiety is
repeated night after night. The small talk conventional at
such affairs, when protracted, may make a demand upon
nervous energies comparable with that required for con-
centrated work. Effort is required of the average individual in order to remain attractive to his associates over a
period of hours. It seems entirely probable that for the
younger set, at least, the tendency to high nervous tension
is increased with the frequent use of alcoholic beverages
and with the common presence of sexual urges. Commonly
in my experience with patients whose social activities have
required an excessive amount of time there has developed
an apparent poise—an outward appearance of calm delib-
erately assumed in order to conceal slight but troublesome
nervous tensions. In spite of much so-called recreation,
the individual fails to secure that degree of relaxation
which it is the purpose of this book to describe.

The doctor or lawyer is an even better example of the

overactive life. When he has little to do, he generally worries tensely, but when this worry is relieved upon the improvement of business, he continues to be tense but in another direction. The reception room now, perhaps, has many patients or clients. Two or more may receive attention at one time. Often the pressure is so great that there is scarcely opportunity to grasp adequately the various narratives of ills or difficulties. Assistants must be employed, their work supervised and their findings considered. At the same time the doctor or lawyer may tensely realize that he is needed elsewhere: at the bedside or operating room, at some special conference or at court.

Teachers at school and at college are frequently no more free from the pressure of modern life. In the grades and in high school they have the task of maintaining discipline in a restive young race. In the colleges those who bear the burdens of executive work frequently find an almost endless detail of matters for decision and action; while those who engage in research in addition to teaching may find their minds active each night for many hours after they have attempted to quit their labors.

No less subject to excess nervous tension are many employees in offices, factories and mercantile establishments. The stenographer who has to write many words per minute in order to get her work out; the salesman or woman standing practically the entire day to serve customers; the factory hand obliged to engage in countless operations to meet the demands of production; the telephone operator alert to make connections for hours at a time—these and many others afford frequent examples of high-tension living. This may be especially evident in particular occupations such as court reporting, type setting or newspaper work in general. Even the farmer, striving to pay taxes and interest and frequently deprived of adequate help by the lure of city life, sometimes feels the strain of too much activity.

Added to the stress of modern occupations are the financial urges from which few are free. Making enough money to satisfy ever increasing desires has come to be an almost constant stimulus to nervous overactivity on the part of working men and women.

No less responsive to the overstimulation of modern times are our youngsters. From infancy through adolescence, as our tissues age and pass from sol toward gel, over-all muscular activities normally tend to decline. The individual ordinarily quiets down. However, under the overstimulation of modern times with each organ of the body more or less affected, the normal trend is often retarded and signs of general excess tension become all too manifest in our youth. Then we note the incessant restlessness in many of our children, their louder, high-pitched voices, their unremitting search for exciting occupations, their addiction to the radio even during hours of study and to the television even when they should be doing something else. No wonder that the overtension of child life today is manifested in a variety of symptoms which some physicians like to call "psychosomatic". These often include nervous habits and tendencies of many forms, including speech disturbances, facial tics, undue fears and other emotional disturbances. Often the child, however bright naturally, suffers in his school work.

On the other hand, in parents modern affairs have as a

rule brought no letup to age-old sources of nervousness of various types: the rearing of children still takes its toll from the nerves of the watchful mother.

Some students point out that it was Rousseau who first asserted that overactivity and rush are distinctive characteristics of the modern era but that he did not prove it; they add that life may have been just as exciting and worrisome in earlier cultures. Support for this objection is found in the evident nervous state even of wild animals in their natural habitats. Furthermore, even in the days of classic Greece, worry was a problem, as shown by the efforts made to develop a philosophy to combat worry; for example, the teachings of the Stoics, including Epictetus. We should be cautious, then, in assuming that other cultures and other ages have been relatively free from tension. But most persons who have lived through the nineties will probably agree that since that time the rush and pressure of events generally have increased in this country, while life on the whole has become more exciting.

Modern invention and labor saving machinery have relieved physical drudgery but apparently have increased the nervous strains. One method to effect relief, at least in part, might be to return to a simpler way of life. But this solution seems impossible; the complexities of modern living evidently are here to stay. It remains to inquire whether science can help us to live more effectively and to enjoy modern civilization without burning the candle at both ends.

2

Tension

How tense we are as a people is rapidly becoming common knowledge. For years we have been reaping a harvest of ulcers and of heart attacks, of nervous and of psychiatric disorders which, as experience is gradually teaching us, has something to do with our states of tension. Even popular opinion often recognizes that overeffort with too much to do can lead to high blood pressure.

However, we Americans have no monopoly on tension states. There was a time, perhaps, when life among Europeans was as quiet as the former chamber music and the pastorals of their great composers might suggest. But that day is long since past. It is now well known that tension states and the disorders mentioned above are by no means limited chiefly to the new world but are prevalent also in the Europe from which most Americans derive. The Yugoslavia of the communists is no exception.

Our activities survive the events that bring them on. When we rise to an occasion we become tense; and when the occasion passes, the momentum tends to continue.

6

This is as true of communities as it is of individuals and explains much in history and in our individual lives. However, when stimulated to increased activity by occasions which pass, the momentum continues but what we do may take on new directions.

Thus America today has been stimulated by participation in two wars in which our very way of life was threatened and one in Korea which awoke us from our dream of disarmament. Gone is the quietude of the nineties when we lived in isolation from the quarrels of Europe, protected by vast oceans. No longer are we isolated. Our attempts to maintain and to spread freedom and our democratic way of life to other lands have survived the wars and are still going on but have aroused strong reactions. For the first time in history, we Americans have become the hated targets of foreign governments, Russia, China, and their satellites, formerly our friends. Their emissaries issue venomous blasts against us in the very New York where we hoped to gather them in a peaceful world organization. Over the radio and by television, we can hear and see them call us "war-mongers" and we read of their threats against our allies of Europe. Our newspapers recount their total preparations for World War III which we must meet or perish. Gone is the quietude of the nineties!

Inevitably, under these conditions, our peaceful hearts are not at rest. As a nation, we build bigger and greater armaments to include guided missiles and other fantastic weapons of atomic warfare designed for massive retaliation. We build radar detection lines, the DEW and others, that we may know earlier of attack by air than we knew

of the surprise attack on Pearl Harbor on the ill-fated
December 7th. No stalwart American doubts that a Rus-
sian attack would meet with successful resistance and a
retaliation which would soon end Kremlin domination of
a slave half-world. But each one of us hopes that it may
never become necessary to achieve by war that consum-
mation, however devoutly to be wished. In the meantime
we live in the shadow of what may be forthcoming. Who
knows?

Thus we are driven on by forebodings of atomic and
hydrogen bombs, but such fears in our people no longer
are what they were. They have subsided in the face of
our ever increasing preparations and resources. Today
most know them not at all, or if at all, then generally un-
consciously. However, our activities in preparation for a
dreaded World War III are not negligible and they constitute an ever present source of national tension.

To some extent they produce this effect because the
great financial cost of national defense against the growing strength of our enemies promotes inflation. Inflation
is a change from present conditions; and any change, if
sufficiently marked, is a stimulus to increased activity, i.e.,
tension. Accordingly our people are possessed of unprecedented large sums of money; and if not of money, then of
credit. This spurs them to buy. They buy and others sell
in unprecedented amounts, while still others manufacture
and build to manufacture more.

The net result is increased tension in the world of business. To be sure it is pleasant tension. Tension can be
pleasant. The efforts to buy and to sell, to build and to
manufacture in increasing amounts can be pleasant. They

can even be necessary. But necessary or unnecessary, pleasant or unpleasant, they still represent tension. We shall come to grips with definitions later.

In this overtense national life of war preparation and of unprecedented industry, each individual tends to participate, whether he knows it or not. We can assume that the hostess at a dinner party, even one who knows little and cares less about foreign affairs and the national economy, is stimulated by the times and acts accordingly, for her actions are in part reactions to the conduct of others whom she meets—and many of these others will move and act with the masses. Truly the influence of national tension on the conduct of each and every individual is impossible to determine; we must leave it to conjecture, albeit cautiously. But at times in our recent history this influence was clearly discernible and it is always reflected in the songs of the day. "Happy days are here again!" was sung jovially if wistfully in the night clubs during the depression in the early thirties. And all participated in one way or another, just as all tend to participate in national activity, whether during a war or the postwar period.

The struggle for existence is fundamental to all explanations of animal life, in groups or individuals. When they say this, biologists no doubt are right, but there is more to it than their words imply. People struggle not only for existence but also to get ahead; often it is to get ahead of each other.

Sometimes the worry is just to keep up—not to fall back. The children must be sent to school, perhaps to college. Shoes cost twice as much as formerly. It is amazing how many and how varied are the financial problems of people living in the most successful country of all time. Worries plus efforts compound their tensions!

Individuals charged with heavy responsibility, accustomed to their work and enjoying it, are likely to show added capacity and prolonged ability to work as long as they are successful. In these times, the heaviest responsibilities fall on statesmen and political executives. According to popular opinion, many of these officials bear their burdens lightly. However, to those close enough to observe them personally, the strains are most evident.

Signs of overstrain can be many and various: the individual may merely show indications of fatigue and added irritability; or he may appear to grow old, acquiring gray hair and added lines and folds in his face; his blood pressure may rise, at least for a time, even if later it falls to former levels. Some persons become unable to fall asleep or else to sleep the night through, while others, with advancing fatigue, fall asleep "as soon as their heads touch the pillow".

Most common among the signs of nervous overstrain (and most easily overlooked by the doctor as due to this cause) are upsets of digestion. If accompanied by fever, diarrhea or vomiting, as often occurs, these nervous upsets are likely to be falsely ascribed to some article of food which was eaten. A diagnosis of ptomaine poisoning is made falsely almost as frequently as it is made at all. The illness, when really present, follows eating decomposing proteins. To be sure, a person in an overtense condition cannot digest comfortably many of the foods which give no trouble under more favorable conditions. To this extent he may be right when he ascribes his distress or bowel disturbance to what he has eaten. But in a larger sense, as we shall see, the seat of his distress lies in an overtense (spastic) digestive tract, which always (in my experience) accompanies conditions of overstrain and which is therefore responsible for his inability to digest foods which would not upset him otherwise. Proper treatment, accordingly, is not primarily dietetic but rather in the direction to which this volume is dedicated.

It is important to avoid nervous breakdowns. That this can be done directly for the first time in history is the present thesis. In many instances, because of neglect, tensions are permitted to build up to a state where control is diminished and nervous disorganization sets in, whereupon a serious turn can develop. However, if each person considers his own organism as part of his business of life, much can be accomplished in prevention as well as in cure.

3

Tension and Heart Attacks

"My neighbor Harry is in the hospital. They say he has had a heart attack!"

Harry, perhaps, is a businessman well-liked by those who know him well. However, Harry could as well be disliked and he could be a factory worker, a lawyer, a doctor, an engineer, an admiral or any other type. Possibly he is forty-five or fifty years old or somewhat older, but he might be only thirty-five. There are many Harries of many ages and this is one reason why I have written this book.

What has tension to do with Harry's heart attack? Let us first consider the case for the defense, namely, that tension has little or nothing to do with bringing it on. Many people, including some doctors and even some heart specialists, still believe this. Currently among these are some who assert that whether Harry has a heart attack or not depends on the state of his coronary arteries, whether these are hardened, sclerotic. Fat, they argue, is deposited in the heart arteries, weakening their walls, thus allowing them to burst or to develop stasis within, so that blood flow to some part of the heart-wall ceases, which is what people know as a heart attack. Arteriosclerosis, they add, is the cause of coronary heart disease and tension plays only a minor role if any. At most, it aggravates the symptoms, these polemists claim, or sets off an attack through an emotional crisis, which would have come a little later on anyway.

Their arguments appear so sound, so scientific, so authoritative that we pause to wonder if they are not wholly right. Without doubt, fatty deposits are found in diseased coronary arteries. What, then, has tension to do with heart attacks? What, indeed?

There was a time when our boys were dying during the war in Korea. Three hundred of them died in combat whose hearts were carefully examined subsequently. Autopsies were performed by Major William F. Enos and his associates. Even though their age averaged in the early twenties, seventy-seven per cent had some degree of disease of the coronary arteries. In many instances, the hearts were so severely diseased that the examiners were amazed. They could not understand how these hearts had held out during the battle until the boy was killed by shot and shell or other external violence.

I do not know of any reasonable way to interpret the findings of Major Enos on these poor boys of ours but that the strain and tension of the war had proved too much for their arteries. Was it their diet? Did their hearts degenerate because they ate too much fat? too much cholesterol?

No record was found and published that could support the view that they had partaken of too much cholesterol.

The Army diet does not provide any excess of fat. Nobody claims that it does. The fat content of meals provided for our Army forces was, we can assume, approximately of the same percentage as was provided for these boys in typical American homes in peacetime. So far as fat content was concerned, these boys had been eating as all Americans eat on the average.

Yet the incidence of severe coronary heart disease in these young boys was very much in excess of the incidence in American boys of the same age who had not participated in the strains and tensions of active warfare. It is said that approximately one out of two American males shows beginning hardening of the coronary arteries at the age of thirty-five or of forty. But what is found in these early-middle-aged men is only the beginnings of disease, not advanced disease such as Major Enos found in many of our three hundred boys. And he found marked coronary heart disease not merely in one out of two but in the majority, namely, in about seventy-seven per cent.

The debaters therefore would find it hard to make out a case to prove that the coronary heart disease found in these fighters post mortem was due chiefly to fatty diet.

Whether or not fatty diet promotes hardening of coronary arteries is still open to question. Opinions and practices differ and the evidence can not be reviewed here.

Perhaps I should indicate my own opinion if only to avert the impression that I am biased. I am not biased against restriction of diet for medical purposes. What is known as the salt-free or salt-poor diet was introduced into medical practice by an article on the subject which I wrote for the Journal of the American Medical Association in 1917. Personally, I have restricted the fats in my own diet since 1912. On the evidence I have not advised the same restriction to my family or to my patients, except where I have found blood cholesterol values high. My own values have never been high and my restriction of fats was for prophylaxis only and on an experimental basis versus the ingestion of substances that might have some bearing on arteriosclerosis and carcinoma.

Accordingly, we can return judicially to Major Enos and quite agree when he writes, "It is most unlikely that one factor alone can be indicated as the cause of coronary sclerosis." We can agree judicially, while pointing out that the evidence for the importance of tension states is quite clear, if only the student does not focus exclusively on one factor alone, such as fat in the diet.

Major Enos concludes that the combatants suffered from *wear and tear* on the lining membranes of the coronary arteries and from *stress* at branching points. While he does not discuss the tense life at war as leading to the wear and tear and stress, his results contrast greatly with what we know of the normal, healthy hearts on the average in American boys in civilian life who have undergone no such strains. It seems safe to assume that their occupation as combatants with its extreme tensions of emotion and effort was largely responsible.

However, we are not yet finished with the debate. There is further reason to believe that students should not divorce tension from their explanations of the origin and development of coronary heart disease.

This is Harry's first heart attack, let us assume, in the sense that his doctor previously found nothing wrong in his heart-record, but now finds that the record indicates that the heart-wall has suffered damage. Nevertheless, Harry may have had heart pains previously, which were misinterpreted as digestive upsets or which were diagnosed as angina.

Doctors like to distinguish angina of the heart from coronary heart disease. Angina is thought of as merely spasm of the coronary arteries, through which the blood runs to supply the heart-wall; while coronary heart disease includes actual hardening and fatty change in those arteries, with resultant damage to sections of the heart-wall if, when and as the blood supply fails.

Angina means pain of a certain squeezing variety as a rule. In a later chapter I shall return to this interesting if gruesome topic. Angina may precede as well as mark the course of coronary heart disease in the form of spells, severe or light. In coronary heart disease, however, the pain may be absent or pass unnoticed. This is why people can die of it suddenly without previous warning.

Spasm of the coronary arteries (or any other artery) *is* tension therein. The circular muscle fibers are shortened persistently and excessively, and this *is* spasm. Throughout this volume, when "tension" is mentioned, it will always have a definite meaning, which may contrast with the vague usage found too often in current literature. Tension will mean the shortening of muscle fibers, which can be reversed. When reversed, the muscle fibers lengthen. This will be known herein as relaxation. All physiologists use the words "tension" and "relaxation" as defined above; at least they do so in their scientific work.

Heart specialists, including our debaters, are inclined to

agree that among the causes of anginal spells are emotional episodes. None would be surprised even if the "organic" attack of Harry followed upon a severe argument with his boss at business, threatening the successful continuation of his career. But those who argue that tension has little or nothing to do with the real causation of Harry's diseased arteries claim that the basis of the disease was already there before his trouble with his boss. In this they are doubtless right. When we point out the apparent significance of tension in the development of coronary heart disease, the argument for this offense does not assume that tension is the one and only cause but only that it evidently plays a role that has been too much neglected. The traditional view of authorities generally has been that coronary heart disease, like arteriosclerosis in general, is of unknown origin, and therefore for the present at least we can do little to prevent it. I take issue with the traditional view because I believe that with better understanding of the role of tension we can do very much to prevent the incidence of coronary heart disease and at the very least can postpone attacks.

This opinion was shared by Dr. John Christiernen, Chief Physician of the Metropolitan Life Insurance Company when that organization began to take interest in the field of tension and relaxation methods some twenty years ago. He became convinced of the magnitude of the role of tension toward developing coronary heart disease with its prime position among cardiovascular diseases as killer number one among the yearly deaths of our population. And as he learned more, he came to believe with me that the key to diminishing this high death rate lies in promulgation among the populace of technical methods of relaxation.

This is why: Without doubt organic characteristics in any individual determine the degree of his susceptibility to any disease, including coronary heart disease. If you are the offspring of two rabbits, there can be no doubt what you are. Inevitably your heredity identifies you and marks you individually for life from all other living creatures. You inherit millions or billions of characteristics, which among other things determine your resistance to heart attacks.

But against every negative there is a positive. What brings on the disease? We cannot yet answer this question in all aspects definitely. But we can throw light on it by comparing our organisms with any man-made instrument or machine. We know that all of these are subject to wear and tear. We can consider what is to most of us the most familiar of machines, the automobile. Cars are turned out at the factories differing in the strength and resistance of their parts. Therefore some suffer damage more than others upon a collision. But in any accident the real cause of the damage never can be found solely in the materials. As a rule much depends upon the manner in which the car was driven. From our familiar experience with damage to cars in collisions, we can learn that the materials in a car do not as a rule suffice to explain the nature and extent of damage sustained in any collision. To explain the damage we must take into account also the nature of the driving or use of the car, whether good or bad. Sometimes poor driving can account for the chief features of the damage sustained. At other times poor materials may explain the chief features, as when a weak or loose fender is knocked off when one car chances slightly to scrape against another.

We must learn to take into account, then, not only the materials but also how we handle our cars, if we would minimize collisions and their ill-effects. Likewise in accounting for any disease, including heart disease, the modern doctor will no longer focus his attention exclusively on our material make-up, whether derived from heredity, diet or other means, but will consider also how we handle ourselves. His reason and his success will thereby be improved. For as we shall see, proper handling of ourselves is the avoidance of undue tension, provided that we live normally otherwise.

By avoiding undue tension, we can do what within us lies to prevent coronary heart disease or at least to slow its development. By conservation of our muscular energies we can save our hearts.

Tension makes demands not only on our hearts but also on our arteries, as will appear presently. After discussing this subject and other matters we shall be better prepared and can return to the subject of heart disease and prevention in the final chapter.

4

Efforts and High Blood Pressure

"Tell me what a person laughs at and I can tell you about him!" is an interesting statement. Better yet, I should say, "Tell me what a person tries to do all day long; tell me what are his efforts, and I can tell you all about him!"

This is a simple statement, but it carries more than appears on the surface. Let us draw open the curtain on you and your efforts. Science can learn much from them. So can you.

You are in bed. It is morning and you are about to awaken to begin the daily trek. There is a slight restless movement of your limbs and trunk, an early sign of return to activity. Your inner world has stirred with a vague meaning to you, a sense all your own. Still in the land of dreams, the world is not yet yours; you have not yet made connections. The movement which you made was your effort to adjust partly to your dreamy state and partly to the dawning world. Possibly it was a response to some noise.

However vague your effort, there was a movement.

Somewhere, perhaps all over, muscles for a moment become overtly active. This was you doing something; this was one of your initial efforts of the day. However vague your experience, however indescribable, you were beginning to return once more to active life. There was a purpose to your stir, if only to change position for greater comfort at the moment.

Soon you open your eyes and look—an effort so slight and habitual as to pass unnoticed. You throw off the bedclothes, slowly or quickly, as is your wont, and you stand. There follow a series of activities which may include washing, selecting and putting on certain clothes, going to the breakfast table, conversing, eating breakfast and perhaps reading the newspaper.

Each of these acts, however minor, are your efforts. Your muscles contract in specific patterns which mark each effort as uniquely as your signature marks you. And you differ in your muscular performance of each act from everybody else, just as does your thumbprint.

All day long you will carry on in a series of efforts within efforts. Whether you are a housewife, a school-girl or a child; whether a businessman, a mechanic or a farmer, this will be true. Whatever your occupation, to be sure, the direction of your efforts will vary. In any event the maze of them will be indescribably complicated. Often you will not know of them at all, as they occur largely mechanized by habit. Often they will shade one into another inseparably, and often you will not even become aware of your efforts and their aims, although very vaguely you will recognize some as yours, marking the significance of your day and your life.

Could you pause for a moment tomorrow and look into this matter of your efforts? What are your aims from moment to moment? Are they really worth-while? What are you trying to accomplish and at what cost? Do you know how to count the costs to you in terms of your energies?

Possibly you will decide then that certain of your major efforts are not really worth-while in their aims. You may determine to discard these but to retain others. Possibly then this will open the way toward the development of new aims and their corresponding efforts. This can mean better organization of your life. If you should really throw some of your customary efforts into the discard, this will result in economy of your nervous energies.

However, you will be aided if you have the "know-how" requisite for observing your efforts. Let us try here to take a first step toward fitting you for this.

Begin with your left arm at rest on the arm of a chair or extended limply on a table. Bend back the left hand at the wrist steadily. Take care not to bend at the elbow.

Notwithstanding this warning, many will bend their arms at the elbow when bending the hand back at the wrist. These persons must practice until they eliminate this. The action of bending back at the wrist is to be the one and only act performed at the moment. This will facilitate observation. Bend steadily for about two or three minutes, to give yourself a good chance to observe a sample of what we have been discussing in the preceding paragraphs. Do not bend the hand inconstantly but keep it steady for the several minutes: do not seesaw. In this you must act as your own monitor, for again, notwithstanding the warning, some will seesaw, thus frustrating the purpose to observe what takes place in you when you bend your hand back steadily.

You should notice a vague sensation in the upper portion of your left forearm. It extends from the wrist, approximately, to the neighborhood of the elbow. At first you may not notice it at all, for it is really delicate and unobtrusive. You may be looking for too much. It is but a misty feeling. But it is there. It marks *you doing:* your effort.

No; not the sensation at the wrist when you bend back your hand. This sensation is clearer and often stronger and easier to recognize than is the delicate sensation at the top of your forearm which marks your effort.

If necessary to help you to observe, close your eyes and try again. Do not look for too much. It will not hit you in the eye. Keep trying to observe the sensation from effort in the top of your forearm when you bend back your hand until you succeed. Thereafter repeat the act frequently. It will help you to know yourself better.

For performing this simple act of bending back at the wrist (which is *not* an exercise) is in a sense like sounding a note on the piano. The note as such is simple and relatively meaningless. Yet of a variety of such notes on the piano in combinations of chords and continuous themes, a concerto is made. The note is the unit.

Likewise the simple act of tension which you have performed is a sample note of your entire life. Put such acts together in combinations over the body which accord with your aims, and you have your life acts of today and of tomorrow.

We do not here engage in idle analysis of you and your

acts. If we hold the microscope up to what you do at each moment it is for the purpose of helping you to live more effectively and perhaps longer. It is to save your energies and thus your health.

"Man", says my distinguished friend Dr. Mervin Kelly of the Bell Telephone Laboratories, "has long studied his physical environment to great advantage. It is time that he should study more about himself!"

I quite agree. Modern science learns much from the study of the minuscule, the minute elements in the physical world. Each molecule, even each atom is found to have important characteristics, differing from others if only in position and rate of movement, but perhaps also even in structure.

Likewise your every activity consists of patterns about which we can learn much. But we must pause to analyze small portions of your acts. Only thus can we understand you and your life.

We return to you bending back your hand, while you observe the sensation in the upper portion of your forearm. This, we repeat, is a sample of you doing. It is your effort. Of such notes is your life composed.

Learn to observe this sensation for yourself. It is called "the feeling of tension", or "tension" for short. If you are a sufficiently good observer, you can find this sensation in the muscles all over your body under your skin at every instant of your life. Your each and every effort will be identified with specific patterns of this sensation, depending upon what muscles you employ to accomplish. What a world of events within events constantly changing in you and in each one of us! Indeed you are a world in yourself, for the complexity of networks of the nerves within you by which you act is comparable with that of the entire network of telephone wires all over the United States! And in your brain, to help power this network, are said to be about ten billion amplifiers, the brain cells.

It is a good thing to know a little about the brain and the nerves, but in daily living you can disregard them. Similarly when you drive a car you do not as a rule need to bother with what goes on under the hood, however important this may be for your car. To go where you wish and when, all you have to do is to see that the wheels turn at the proper rate and in the required direction. In daily living your muscles correspond to the wheels. Properly directed, they will tend to take you where you wish to go in life, in so far as this is possible.

However, there may be times when wheels turn too fast for your own good. And the direction may be all wrong. Some people exceed the speed limit in their muscle traffic. If you are one of these, you may be a candidate for high blood pressure.

The reason is not far to seek. In all of your efforts, muscles contract. Shortening of muscle fibers depends on a chemical change within the fibers. It is a combustion or fire; energy is used up. Heat is given off. For a fire there must be fuel and oxygen. The fuel is blood sugar in part. Where can the muscle get these supplies but from the blood stream through the muscle? Nowhere else. Accordingly every time you tense a muscle, you are making a demand (however slight) on the heart for more pressure in the blood stream and more circulation in the muscle. Also the little arteries in the muscle automatically respond to this demand by tension increase in their muscular walls.

What a complex mechanism Nature has achieved in us! But I have greatly oversimplified the picture. For every time we make an effort, no matter how slight, the fires in muscular contraction result in ashes and waste products. We need not list these products of muscle activity or metabolism. They must be carried away from the muscle in which they are produced, else they will clog it. There will be excessive fatigue. Where is the ash remover to be found but the blood stream? Nowhere else. In this respect also, every time you tense a muscle you are making a demand on your heart and arteries for higher pressure and more circulation.

A single movement is of course inconsequential. By itself it does not raise the blood pressure noticeably, any more than a single vote determines the results of a national election. But each tension, like each vote, counts toward a final result.

Thus, if we are overtense during much of the day, if our efforts are excessive (whatever their purposes), we are in effect asking for higher blood pressure.

Our effort-circuits, in other words, are overactive and make excessive demands on our hearts and blood vessels.

Fortunately, the hearts and blood vessels in many of us are so well fortified against excessive demands on them that no noticeable ill results. The heart pumps a little harder, the vessels contract a little more, but no chronic high blood pressure is noted. Such fortunate persons have good heredity. Inquire of them and perhaps you will discover that their parents, grandparents and other near relatives mostly were free from histories of high blood pressure and coronary heart disease.. Possibly good heredity means that the fortunate ones were born with good materials in their heart and blood vessels, including the "elastin" in their arteries.

We do not know what good heredity really means in the sense of inborn materials. However, if one or both parents died with hypertension or coronary heart disease or if your brothers or sisters show signs of these disorders, it is well to be more careful. You may be among those who are more susceptible to developing high blood pressure. Then you would do well to learn to be more relaxed.

Undue alarm is to be avoided, however. Going to the doctor and learning that your pressure is somewhat elevated in a single test may have little significance. Perhaps you were nervously excited, that is, unduly tense during the test. Prior to an operation, for example, this can occur in people who never really develop chronic high blood pressure. Measurements should be repeated fairly frequently before any conclusion is reached that a person suffers from what is called "essential hypertension".

When you make any effort whatsoever, then, your muscles contract in distinctive patterns and time phases which accord with your aims. Your brain and your nerves participate but also your heart and your blood vessels in each and every effort-circuit (as I have called the body process). This is not the whole story. There is more to be said in the following chapter.

5

Anxiety

Anxiety is not limited to older people. It occurs at all
ages. During World War II, a number of cadets under
training for the air arm of the U.S. Navy showed signs of
strain, including instances commonly called "nervous
breakdowns".

It was no wonder. Abrupt changes in life can be hard to
bear. Fresh from their homes and their schools, youths
of nineteen to twenty-two or thereabouts were being disci-
plined to fly and service planes for purposes of war against
the Germans and the Japanese. At times they were exposed to dangers new and unfamiliar. The future offered
little security. Yet there was no choice. Retreat to home
was impossible, unthinkable.

To meet the problem, the U.S. Navy sent five officers
mostly of commander rank to the Laboratory for Clinical
Physiology in Chicago to be trained as instructors in scientific relaxation. They were not doctors, and therefore there
was no design to prepare them to treat nervous illness.
Besides the strictly medical department in the field of
scientific relaxation which is for doctors and for doctors

alone, there is also a department for educators. Good teachers in our schools and colleges, we believe, could do much to improve our daily habits of living. However, they must have received preparatory training in scientific relaxation (and this means something quite different from reading unauthorized books on the subject). Navy authorities evidently understood.

Because of war urgency, an intensive course of training to be teachers was provided for the "Navy Five", as they called themselves. They could afford only six weeks' time in Chicago. Hours for lectures and discussion were quickly arranged so that they could know what were the purposes and objectives of the training course and how they could teach the cadets effectively. But scientific relaxation is not just lying down or sitting up in quiet manner with good intentions. It is as technical an undertaking as running a plane, which many of the cadets were striving to learn. Accordingly, on each day of their course except Sundays, in three different periods lasting one hour apiece, the Navy Five were trained to relax. In some periods they lay on couches; in others, however, they sat up or they stood. They needed to acquire skill in relaxation themselves in order to transmit such skill to others.

But to acquire technical skill of any kind generally requires not only professional instruction but also practice on the part of the pupil. Accordingly into a day already full, we had to crowd two additional hour periods for them to practice on what they were being taught. Furthermore, we had to provide for tests to know whether they were really learning.

For this I had designed electronic apparatus. I had been

very fortunate in having the benevolent cooperation of the Bell Telephone Laboratories in this difficult electronic field and was greatly indebted for this to Dr. Mervin Kelly, the President, and to his predecessors in this office.

One hour per day was provided for testing how relaxed each of the Five was becoming. The tests showed that they were really learning.

Five or six hours per day of rest with muscles really relaxed, following a night of sleep, is a lot of rest for any healthy person, and therefore a balance had to be provided. This was especially necessary since the Navy Five were rugged athletes, some of them athletic coaches of national fame. We needed to keep up the daily exercise which had long been their habit. Therefore, at least once a day, each of the Navy Five engaged in vigorous athletics at the local Y.M.C.A. Thus they developed fatigue products which enabled them to relax more readily during the training hours in the Laboratory.

They learned, however, that physical exercise has little relationship to technical relaxation. Athletics, we can agree, need no justification; they are part and parcel of a vigorous and healthy life. But relaxation skills are as applicable to the habits of sedentary people as to athletes. These skills have to do not only with the muscular exercise visible in athletics but quite as much with the invisible muscular activities which constitute our daily efforts. Until this is widely understood, many people will identify relaxation skill with physical exercise or the results. According to my experience, those who preach "relaxation exercises" have not quite understood that to relax is simply *not* to do; it is the total absence of any muscular exercise.

Understanding these matters, the Navy Five returned to the pre-flight schools in various parts of the United States. They trained ninety-five other officers to be teachers, making a total of one hundred relaxation officers. Within a period of the first seven months, 15,700 cadets received training. The results were published by Commander William Neufeld in the *American Journal of Psychiatry.* He reported evidence that, as a consequence of the training, states of nervousness and fatigue were reduced in incidence, sleep was improved and accident-rate lowered as compared with groups who had not received relaxation training. There was considerable enthusiasm among many who had participated as pupils but also among untrained officers and others who had the opportunity to observe the cadets.

Thus, according to the evidence, anxiety among cadets was on the whole diminished. Even so, they continued at their daily training to fit them for air combat. What can we learn from this and other studies as to the real causes of anxiety?

Popular opinion has it that anxiety is created by whatever troubles us. Thus a man whose position is in jeopardy may be deeply concerned about his prestige and about supporting his family. Or a mother may worry about the illness of her child. Similarly, according to popular opinion, the anxiety of the cadets was *caused* by the dangers, present and future, in learning to fly for combat.

Like many other popular views, there is some logical basis for the prevalent opinion that anxiety (where it does not concern personal health) generally is caused by external circumstances and situations. If I am startled upon the occurrence of a sudden noise, there is at least a partial justification for the belief that the noise caused the jump which I exhibited. If the noise had not occurred, I would not have jumped. But a scientific study disclosed that people are less startled or not at all if their muscles are generally relaxed. The individual exhibits the jump or startle reaction only if and when he is tense. What really happens, therefore, is that the startle merely is touched off or triggered by the noise. The noise acts as stimulus only, and there is a great difference between *stimulus* and *cause*. The cause of the startle or jump thus really is in large part the tenseness in the individual. When he is not tense, he is not disturbed by the noise emotionally.

If this is true, people generally have labored on a partly false impression about their concerns, fears and anxieties. Attributing the onset of these states solely to situations which are met, to the hardships or future hardships of life, has been a great popular mistake, which needs to be corrected in the interests of better living.

Ministers, priests and rabbis agree that without hardships such as lead toward anxiety, life would be drab. To meet trials and tribulations develops courage and character. It can make for higher spiritual development. Yet, this view, to which I heartily agree, does not go along with the view that the same trials and tribulations are the causes of our concerns and anxiety; for if they were the real causes, there would be nothing that we could do about our conduct. We would be the slaves of the situations which confront us.

I must confess that to a large extent people act as if they really were slaves. Their false beliefs confine them in intellectual concentration camps. But there is a way out to freedom, whereof I would speak in the present volume.

Let me illustrate. But yesterday I was met by a man whose respect for the golden rule has been voiced and demonstrated in his business life. Yet he was emotionally upset, concerned over criticisms of his conduct, which led him to consider suicide as an escape and which led a psychiatrist to suggest a three-months stay in a mental hospital.

He regarded the criticisms levelled against him as the *cause* of the emotional disturbance which his facial expression revealed. Obviously, if these criticisms were really the cause, there was nothing much he could do for himself to improve his emotional condition. He was helpless. Therefore he thought of suicide, and the psychiatrist thought of shock treatment.

But there *was* something he could do about it. The first step was to correct the false belief which held him helpless. The situation which he faced was really unpredictable in its possible developments. No one could prophesy whether the future really held the ill for him which he feared. What he needed to do first of all was to appraise the situation objectively.

However, an overtense person tends to be ill-qualified to render objective judgments about matters over which he is disturbed emotionally. He fails to display what is known as the "judicial temperament". As he becomes relaxed, in my experience, his reasoning about such matters tends to improve. He sees things in a colder, clearer light.

Let me illustrate again; this time with a married woman whose anxiety was not reasonable, as was that of the man mentioned, but was so unreasonable as to indicate mental disorder. For several years, she related, she had been severely depressed over her "life-span". Worry had consumed her energies, both day and night. She was fifty years old, she said, and she could not endure this. Her life with her husband was successful. Their circumstances were less than comfortable; but they managed to get along.

To become fifty years old obviously is part of the normal state of healthy man and woman. You are not then what you once were; but if this stimulates you to unceasing worry, presumably there is something wrong with you rather than with your span of life.

The woman in question (whom I shall call Mrs. Hardy) said this of her own initiative. Other women were fifty and did not worry about their span of life until they became unfit for household and social duties, as she did. Therefore, she added, there certainly was something the matter with her mind. She knew that her anxiety was foolish, unreasonable, but "she could not stop worrying". She "must be headed for the psychopathic hospital!" What would become of her and her family? What did the future hold? She wept miserably.

Was this what is called a mental disorder of the menopause? Perhaps. However, it had not begun when menstruation ceased and did not have certain earmarks of menopause psychosis, as I know them.

In either case, what is the cause of such depression? The question as thus worded assumes that there is just one cause. This assumption generally is not justified when one deals with disorder in so complex an organism as the human.

If the question means, "What was wrong in her brain or elsewhere in her body?" it is a good question and deserves a straightforward answer. Speaking for myself alone, after a lifetime of experience I can answer simply about anxiety states of this particular type: "I do not know". I have no theory whether there was brain defect or insufficiency or glandular or metabolic disease or none of these to induce her toward the irrationality mentioned. I know of no psychiatric theory which really affords a key to understanding what has gone wrong; but there are theories which are widely accepted.

Fortunately, however, experience has taught me the means and technique toward correction of different types of anxiety states, whether rational or somewhat irrational. For this, thanks are due to scientific relaxation methods, but they are highly technical.

By these means, Mrs. Hardy was instructed step by step to recognize when and where she was tensing muscles at each moment of her life. She practiced faithfully and became expert at this art of recognition. Gradually she learned to distinguish between what she was tense about (i.e., her age) and her tension. Her tension could be felt by her variously in the sundry parts of her body. When she was particularly depressed, she could note a characteristic "heavy" feeling in the chest and abdomen, affecting breathing. She learned the mark of tension as distinguished by the sensation which the reader observed (I hope) upon bending back the hand at the wrist. This

sensation appeared in the upper portion of the forearm
when the hand was bending back at the wrist. She employed this sensation as a criterion for recognizing tension;
somewhat as a shopper takes along a swatch or sample of
a color of cloth which she wishes to match in a larger
piece for purchase and use.

Thus learning, the day came when she began to realize
that her life-span would not trouble her if she were not
excessively tense. When troubled, she now became able
to notice when and where she was contracting muscles,
being tense unnecessarily. Her efforts to adapt herself to
her daily responsibilities were found to be extreme. She
was trying so hard that she really failed to meet her life
situations successfully.

Accordingly, she practiced at being more relaxed not
only during periods lying down, but also during her
housework, during her communications with family members and others as well as during her entire daily life. She
learned step by step how to relax differentially.

Thus she saved her energies.

Specifically, she learned that when she engaged in
anxiety about her age and life-span, she was no mere
puppet obliged to perform this act by external mechanical
or other forces. On the contrary, although she had not
been aware of it, it was she who had been actively performing in a manner which could have but one result,
namely anxiety.

She learned from her own skilled observation, once this
had been developed, that at any moment of anxiety, *it was
she doing*. She was doing something with her muscles just
as definitely as if she were sweeping a room or washing

the dishes. Anxiety was an act which (at least in part) she was performing but need not perform.

She was helped to realize this in moments when she had become relatively free from tension in her muscles. This occurred for the first time when she was lying down in practice. To her surprise, perhaps, for the first time in years she found herself free for the moment from the severe anxiety which previously had oppressed her constantly.

To her it was an amazing experience! For the moment and briefly thereafter it afforded her insight and a certain degree of hope. But in the disease from which she suffered, hope is an uncertain light. It flickers and is soon extinguished.

The doctor must know this and, oddly enough, should be careful not to speak to one with such disease encouragingly. Like a child suffering from inanition—perhaps dying, but unable to partake of the nourishment he needs— so the psychotic depressive tends to react with more depression to any marked encouragement offered in speech.

With little or no encouragement, therefore, but prompted to practice, Mrs. Hardy learned to save her muscular efforts to solve problems about her age. She came to realize that the greater her efforts to solve these problems, the worse was her condition. She had meant well; her intentions had been good. But, as she was informed, the adage applied to these efforts was "Good intentions pave the road to hell!"

By learning to go negative in her efforts to solve her problems regarding her advanced age, she gradually acquired insight, confidence and self-control. She became free from the fears that had held her a slave. She became confident, self-assured and cheerful. Measurements of her tension state confirmed her improvement by objective tests. She returned fully to her household duties, sustained financial trials with emotional calm when her husband met with financial difficulties and became able to help him in his business. It was believed that she now was free from nervousness, to a degree never before seen in her, even during younger years.

How can I explain so striking a result when I do not claim that research has as yet enabled us to understand the body state in cyclothymic disease? The interpretation seems to lie close at hand. Whatever the disease, whether we understand it fundamentally or not, saving our energy should in principle enable us to withstand it more successfully. This was accomplished in the case of Mrs. Hardy.

6

Anxiety and Ulcers

In the public opinion, anxiety is closely linked to ulcers of the stomach and adjacent intestine. However, I know of no proof that this variety of tenseness is more productive of ulcer than are other varieties. Mrs. Hardy had not developed an ulcer; nor had many other of the Mrs. Hardys whom I have seen.

Perhaps the businessman who alternates between the tensions of hope and of uncertainty gets ulcers more frequently. There are no reliable statistics on these matters. Certain psychiatrists have developed theories about the type of personality that eventuates in ulcer; but no real evidence has been presented.

The story is this. During the early nineteen-twenties, medical opinion generally attributed the origin of these ulcers to infection. Toward the end of this decade in a book called *Progressive Relaxation* addressed to doctors, I suggested that they might better look to the tense state of the individuals who developed this type of malady. As yet there was no proof. This was to a large extent furnished in later years when Lester Dragstedt and other surgeons

cut the vagus nerve in cats which leads to the stomach
and adjacent intestines and spurs them on to activity.
Deprived of this incoming wire, this section of the digestive tract relaxed and the ulcer tended to heal and there
was less recurrence. Less acid was secreted also, and the
burning several hours after a big meal which marks an
ulcer was lessened or disappeared.

Here was proof. However, the prior success of my suggestion often leads me to wish that matters which I have
really proved would find as ready acceptance.

Be that as it may, current medical opinion generally
agrees that the nervous, overzealous individual with his
anxieties is a good candidate for "ulcers". Why this appears to be true can be discussed in this chapter.

In the overtense person, it would seem, the stomach
churns overtime and the acidity runs high. The lining of
the stomach is protected against ulcer formation by substances locally present, not wholly known as yet. When
the wall becomes overtense, I venture to suggest, circulation is impaired because the blood vessels therein are
squeezed unduly. But adequate circulation is necessary
for the protection of any tissue; in the absence thereof,
irritants tend to provoke ulcer formation. This is merely a
theory; but it suggests an order of research to answer an
important question.

There is another matter which calls for thought. How
can we explain the association of ulcer with the presence
of habitual overtenseness in daily life? Why do overtense
business executives, for instance, suffer therefrom so frequently?

According to my impression (founded on lengthy clini-

cal experience which nevertheless falls short of proof),
the stomach shares the excesive tension when we engage
in undue efforts in our daily lives. My teacher, the distinguished Walter B. Cannon of Harvard, first demonstrated in cats the "spastic" state of the stomach when in
the presence of dogs. Anger stopped digestion. The words
"tense" and "tension" were not yet in vogue, for in the
first decade of this century the scientific relaxation of these
pages had not yet been developed.

Now we can say clearly that the cat which sees the
dog becomes tense all over, in each and every muscle.
Externally we see her back arching; her fur stands on end,
her pupils enlarge, various glands pour out secretions,
doubtless including epinephrine, her blood pressure rises,
she becomes prepared for flight or fight. She hisses, spits
and scratches.

It is no time for digestion. This is an emergency! Something must be done at once! The whole organism is called
into action, just as might occur in a nation suddenly alerted
for war!

It is a time for decision, as are all emergencies. Decision
by an individual, whether of the cat or of the human
family, depends upon how the situation faced is pictured.
We might express this as follows (I do not pose as an expert in the cat language). "This dog certainly has no
business on earth; not here in my presence, anyway! I
might scratch his eyes out!" (Arches back, hisses, spits.)
"Or perhaps it would be better to beat a safe retreat!"

If the cat has no such diction, as might be admitted
freely, she nevertheless must evaluate her chances. Per-

haps she "has no stomach for a fight". It is notorious that human beings may vomit before a battle.

Objectively, we know, the cat prepares externally and internally to act in the emergency. What I am here trying to add to this well-known fact is that any individual evaluates the situation which he faces, and my added theory is that the stomach walls participate in the evaluation.

Sensations from these walls certainly are present whenever I evaluate any situation or problem, for I can observe them readily. Without them, the matters with which I deal hold less interest and become devoid of color.

The sensations from the stomach walls are delicate indeed and pass unnoticed except to the highly trained observer. I have been self-trained but in earlier years have tried to pass on this type of training to university professors of psychology.

It is a fascinating field, this internal picturing which, unknown to any but the highly trained, passes our understanding and our common observation. Yet without the fine, delicate sensations which make it possible for human beings to evaluate what they experience, life would be vapid.

I have been speaking herein of an unknown world. Those who never have observed within had better skip these paragraphs, for they will mean little or nothing. As little, perhaps, as would discussions of the use of atomic energies have meant to the physicists of a bygone age!

The tenseness in our digestive tracts, then, I believe, is part and parcel of our actions and reactions to the situations and problems when we meet them with excessive effort. Externally, the tenseness can mean indigestion, tending to ulcer formation or other stomach ills. Internally to us, there are unpleasant sensations which, like the shadows in a painting or the threatening notes in music, picture an uncertain world.

Thus unawaredly we are artists within. Sometimes in our phantasies we picture a future life with no hardships to face; angels on a cloud, we play on our little harps with eternal placidity. Then there will be no growling stomachs, no ulcers!

Meanwhile, we have practical lives to lead. In this it is best for us to picture and evaluate the unpleasant in life, the menaces and the possible alternatives. For this purpose, our internal pictures (be we cat or man) need to be true, rather than always pleasant. Only as angels can we afford always to picture a perfect world.

Rather, it is a hard world which we face, often dangerous, sometimes calamitous. We should know this, for best conduct and for survival. In this, our digestive tract helps with its ever varying sensations of comfort and discomfort.

When there is distress or pain therefrom, it is time to take heed lest our energies be depleted by needless efforts and we develop "ulcers"!

7

Fears and Success

"Success" is a word commonly used by businessmen and the populace. It is eschewed by biologists. They prefer the expression "adjustment to environment". Thus they hold the organisms which they study at a respectful, academic distance.

Whether or not smaller organisms such as those which elude the naked eye really have "feelings" is a remote speculation. When, for example, a jelly-like but living cell such as the amoeba (which frequents our intestines in benign or injurious forms) approaches a particle of food and engulfs it, whatever the "feelings", if any, there is an act that makes for sustenance and survival. In the practical terms of the populace, the little organism has achieved a certain "success".

The amoeba moves about gelatinously, so to speak. Having no muscles, it flows with the aid of hair-like appearing processes, known as "cilia". Its attempts as an organism toward survival are commonly regarded as mechanisms forcing its actions; but ours have often been regarded likewise. I have no view on the matter concerning the amoeba.

44

However, these movements toward sustenance, as well as others away from harmful conditions, can be regarded as the prototypes of what occurs in us. Like the amoeba we move not only to survive ("to adjust to environment") but also to improve our status in one respect or another. We make efforts, for we have muscles. In the course of evolution from the one-cell stage of our progenitors, as is believed, muscles came to be developed. There was differentiation of function among our tissues. No longer were all of our functions performed in and by one cell, which was our sole but undifferentiated being. On the contrary, our cells began to differentiate and to engage in a division of labor (to employ the current expression).

Muscles came to be the effectors of our efforts. We acquired a brain which became highly developed but which always in each section retained a more or less direct connection with a specific section of muscle. Thus our internal communicating system (our nerves) could act and does act always in unison with our muscles, the effector organs of our lives. Such has been the division of labor accomplished in the course of evolution.

Was Darwin right in ascribing such vast internal enterprises to "natural selection and the survival of the fittest"? This is a passing question, which, however fascinating and important, cannot be discussed here.

Let us boldly seek a definition for "success" which can encompass what the biologist reservedly contemplates when he speaks of "adjustment to environment" as well as what the layman means by "success" in any enterprise. Let us go further and agree to use the term to mean the achievement of the result of any effort which we make at any moment of the day! We need such a word for present purposes, and logic permits us to employ it accordingly; for logic depends upon agreements and proceeds therefrom.

When you utter any sentence whatsoever, for example, we shall regard this as indicating a certain success. Perhaps you have never regarded speech as a successful endeavor, but I know of stammerers and stutterers whom I have taught who are vividly aware that when they speak without difficulties, their efforts have met with success! Furthermore those who taught you to speak during infancy doubtless watched your early efforts for signs of success.

I will not belabor the point. But when man strives for success, the processes are intricate beyond description. He pictures the future with the drawing materials which he has derived from his past experience added to his instinctual proclivities. He tries to solve problems of living successfully. For solving problems, meeting situations, the picturing is pre-requisite. Representation of any kind whatsoever, when performed by man, is part and parcel of the effort for success. Science is but the result of group effort to represent correctly.

In the broadest sense of the word, fear marks every effort to meet situations successfully. The emotion in full blossom is exemplified when cat meets dog. Marked fears occur when our lives are endangered, as when the doctor tells us we may have or have cancer, heart disease, high blood pressure or some other alarming disease. Some people live in chronic fearfulness of such states, with various degrees of justification.

Others live in chronic fearfulness of losing their jobs,

their social position, their money or other matters which they regard as of value.

Many people have fears which they do not even voice. A woman sitting in her living-room while watching television wonders frequently whether some intruder may appear at the window. A man watches every expression of his boss wondering which is favorable, which unfavorable.

Fears may mount and become habitual. Sometimes they are pathological.

One woman of about thirty-two years suffered from unreasonable fears of various kinds since the age of twelve. Constantly during her waking hours she lived in a background of fear. She was married and lived with her husband. They had several children. However, she developed fears of stabbing one or another of them to death, and by this her life was rendered uncertain and miserable.

As a measure of protection, she tried to leave knives and other weapons out of sight. Nevertheless the fears of homicide had been severe for years.

Under instruction, she undertook to learn how to control herself emotionally. She readily acquired facility in observing her tension states, their locale and their passing variety. She noted that when she made efforts to hide knives, she really was exerting herself in the interests of security. But like her other well-intentioned efforts, the results were only to worsen her fears. In seeking to protect herself against fearful situations, she only plunged in deeper.

Accordingly she learned to abandon these efforts to solve her fear problems. As she became more relaxed, she became less fearful. Her fear states lost the momentum which had characterized them since childhood. Her habits became modified for the better. After she had become more relaxed, she failed to report about her fear states when we met for instruction. After waiting for a word about them which did not come, I asked directly. She replied, "I have not been interested in them any more! I have attended to other things".

Her confidence was as striking as her nonchalance. I had promised her nothing in therapeutic results, but had emphasized that the task of learning would depend upon her alone. My function would be only to provide instruction. She must do the rest.

Thus, so far as possible, I had avoided what is called "suggestion". There is good reason for this. Therapeutic suggestion is known for the inconstancy and uncertainty of its results. Over a period of time the same defects apply to methods of hypnosis.

In my opinion there is further objection to reliance upon methods of suggestion and hypnosis. They associate actions and reactions of the patient to the doctor or other individual who issues the suggestions or commands. In a sense they foster mechanisms of personality rather than freedom of choice. I have witnessed unhealthful results.

Accordingly, in the approach to this patient (like others in my clinic), suggestive methods are cautiously avoided. Teachers of scientific relaxation are trained likewise in precaution.

We undertook a unique experiment in this study. Whereas severe anxiety states allied with compulsive fears in the past have generally required scores of hours of instruction, I wondered whether it would be possible in this case at least to abridge the course.

This patient learned to control her fears after only eleven hours of technical instruction. Four weeks were allowed for practice after each hour. Judging from the skill at observation and emotional control which she has exhibited, the fears may never return. However, when last I saw her, only two months had elapsed since she became well. We must plan to wait for years to come if we would test the permanence of the results.

In the meantime, to say the least, she is living more comfortably. She has learned to relax her fear states.

8

Tense Persons

In the rush of the present day, man has in part forgotten how to live. Joy in sunlight, birds and flowers
is left chiefly to the poet; delight in line and curve is
sought in the studio; while interest in circumstance becomes the special task of the dramatist. This deficiency in
modern living seems at least partly due to the fact that
the appreciation of beauty as well as doing things beauti-
fully demands a certain abandon. Lacking this, it would
seem, many persons, defeated in the purposes of their
special pursuits, become discontented—even to the point
of suicide.

Modern living often is found wanting not merely artis-
tically but also economically. In its broadest sense, economy pertains to whatever is of value. To count costs chiefly
in terms of dollars is a form of materialism dominant in
many parts of Western civilization. Few persons care
how much they spend in terms of nervous and mental
energy. When healthy they are likely to take their daily
pursuits with a seriousness and intentness that would be
warranted only if they were immortal. Evidently, a saner

grasp on reality occurs when it is recognized that energies commonly wasted might, with the same accomplishment, be saved.

During rush and other activities involving a considerable expenditure of energy, any individual, as can readily be observed, shows signs that he is markedly contracting muscles in various parts of his body. We say that he is tense. Among your friends you can no doubt recognize some who are tense too much of the time. I should like to introduce several interesting examples as met by the physician.

First is a friendly sort of man—evidently alert, energetic and intellectual. He seems to be about thirty-seven years old and is married but childless. He is a professor and is known as a hard worker. As he chats, you note that he wrinkles his forehead often and that he holds his eyes wide open. Watching carefully, you see that he shifts some part of his body from time to time, evidently in order to make it more comfortable. Aside from these inconspicuous signs, he does not impress you as an example of a tense person until you hear his account of himself. When a student at college, he relates, he was under severe mental strain. He found himself continually thinking about his work day and night. Never a sound sleeper, he then, for the first time, began to pass many sleepless hours during the night. Particularly during the last decade, he has felt tense and has not rested well. A medical examination has failed to disclose any serious abnormality. Nevertheless he mentions a certain lassitude—a fatigue, which he states has detracted from his mental efficiency.

Another illustration is a lovely lady of about forty. She

is well-to-do, manages her household and four children with the aid of one maid, often does without a nurse and still finds time to meet her social acquaintances, to serve on committees and to keep her figure lithe and agile through ballet practice. She meets this continual run of duties with outward poise, except that she is occasionally cross with the children. But she admits that she frequently feels excited and irritable and that she is full of fear when she addresses a gathering or undertakes social responsibilities. Of late she has not slept very well and at times has had nausea with frontal headaches. Like the gentleman depicted above, she has no disease that need worry her, no disorder except, obviously, her nervous and mental habits. You notice that she speaks somewhat fast and a little too much. She looks at you with eyes fairly wide open, and her expression changes frequently, as she frowns or wrinkles her forehead. Occasionally she shifts her limbs or sighs. On the whole, however, she sits fairly quietly, and it is the recital of her experiences rather than her behavior that first brings to your notice that she, also, is a tense person.

Here is a tall, well-built man, about forty-eight years old. He has the keen eye of the business executive who sizes you up at a glance. His voice is quiet and controlled, and you look in vain for outward evidences of restlessness or fidgets. However, there is something about him that makes you feel that he is tense, overalert, "just waiting to go". Like his competitors, at the present time of intense activity, he has business worries; in fact, he finds himself unable to cease thinking about his affairs. But he had similar difficulties during easier times and has often wished that he could master his business in the sense of letting it take its course, rather than being continually concerned about it. An examination discloses no disease of heart, kidneys or thyroid gland. When you learn that he does not sleep well, frequently has one or more loose bowel movements per day and that his blood pressure has been high, you wonder whether these symptoms are not in some way connected with his mental characteristics.

A young lady of twenty-five shows signs which will not be hard to read. She is a stenographer, and if you watch her at work you note that she holds her back and neck somewhat stiffly. At times she almost wriggles, as if to get herself into a more comfortable position, while she frowns, wrinkles her forehead or sighs as if worried or distressed. She scarcely sits still for as long as a minute, always finding occasion to move some part of her body, such as a hand or a leg. You do not feel at rest while speaking with her. You are not surprised to hear her say that she is nervous and chronically fatigued, because evidently there is no minute of the day when she is even partially at rest. Doubtless she has always been inclined to be nervous; for instance, she recalls that once, after a cyclone had been predicted, she awakened during a strong wind to find herself trembling all over. During the same year, while on a voyage to Europe, a similar trembling spell set in, this time without apparent reason. Since then she has had such spells at irregular intervals. However, her life was relatively uneventful until two years ago, when she nursed her father, who was dying of heart disease. A year later an insurance examiner informed her that she had heart leakage. This continued to worry her greatly, until she developed a feeling of terror, which was not assuaged when specialists informed her last fall that her heart was quite normal. Following this spell of fright about her own condition, she had various pains, which made her all the more fearful. Her appearance no less than her recital leaves the careful observer in no doubt that she has been in a state of high tension.

I might continue indefinitely to introduce further instances and varieties of symptoms; for, as is known, every organ in the body is supplied with nerves which, when overactive, produce effects deviating from normal. Suppose instead we now accompany John Doe, who is habitually very tense, in a typical attempt to find a better adjustment to life.

Perhaps Mr. Doe visits a very good doctor, who is accustomed to look chiefly for clear-cut pictures of pathological changes in tissues. The doctor concludes that there is nothing seriously wrong and refers the matter to a neurologist. This specialist makes another examination and, as before, finds "no pathology". The nerves are all structurally intact. He tells Mr. Doe, "There is nothing the matter with you. Go home and forget it!"

Mr. Doe tries to follow the advice. He feels relieved because both doctors have said that there is nothing seriously the matter. But the symptoms continue, or soon return, interfering with his work and happiness, and he begins to wonder what to do next.

An instance which brings out the present point amusingly was related thirty years ago by a professor of psychology. At the beginning of the school year a man came to his office asking, "Have you any courses in forgetting?"

"We have a course on memory", answered the professor, "but no one has ever asked for a course on forgetting. What do you want one for?" "Well", answered the man, hesitating, "I have been sick for many years, and a neurologist examined me and told me not to worry but just to forget it. I tried to but couldn't; so I thought maybe you might have some course to teach me how to forget." In telling this story, the professor laughed heartily; however, he evidently felt that the laugh was not altogether on the patient, but also in some measure on the neurologist who did nothing to relieve the patient's suffering, simply because he had found no pathological change in structure.

Returning to Mr. Doe, he tends to go from physician to physician, feeling that he has not been understood. If told that his suffering is only imaginary, he becomes greatly puzzled, because to him it seems very real. Perhaps he comes upon a physician who maintains that nervousness always is caused by some organic disease and who discovers something that has previously been overlooked, for example, infected tonsils. Thereupon the tonsils are removed, and the patient awaits the clearing up of the many symptoms he has long endured. But this hope also may eventually be followed by disappointment. For it has never been proved that nervous irritability and excitement can result from infections in the absence of fever and distress.

New hope arises if he finds a physician who believes that the symptoms are due to glandular trouble. Perhaps a test is made of the air he expires and it is found that he consumes less oxygen than is normal for his age, sex and weight. In common parlance, his fires are burning a little low; in medical terms, his basal metabolic rate is below normal. The conclusion is drawn that his thyroid gland is not "up to par"; to help matters along he takes some glandular substance from a sow or other stockyard animal each day. The substance given may be from the thyroid or from another gland, such as the pituitary or the suprarenal. Thanks to this daily dose Mr. Doe feels new "pep" and less fatigue. He concludes that he is on the way to the answer. Both doctor and patient may become well pleased when a later test shows that the basal metabolic rate has become higher.

In many instances, however, the wave of optimism soon subsides. Notwithstanding the "lift" due to the thyroid substance, his efficiency again suffers a letdown. Palpitation may set in, for the medication may stimulate a tired heart unduly. Both doctor and patient may find that when fatigue is present, whether recognized or not, stimulation of a wearied apparatus by thyroid preparations is only a make-believe route toward cure. Thyroid can stimulate like coffee and can seem to dissipate fatigue; it has its place at times, but does not prove of lasting service when the chief complaint derives from excessive wear and tear on the nervous and muscular systems and on the blood vessels.

If John Doe's fires burn low, perhaps they have been set so by some form of regulatory apparatus such as controls many other functions, including how warm we become or how much and what we eat. We can suspect that such an apparatus exists, even if it is as yet unproved; for the body tends in many ways to provide regulations for undue expenditure of energy when wear and tear have

proved excessive. It is a plausible hypothesis that the
thyroid regulator tends to be set low when fatigue becomes excessive. The combination of fatigue with low
basal metabolism is a familiar one in my experience, and,
as fatigue disappears with healthful rest, tests often show
a change toward normal rates.

To be sure, if the patient has become thoroughly imbued
with the *belief* that the medical measures, whatever they
are, have removed the cause of his long sufferings, his
feelings may be so greatly affected as to result in some
improvement in his general symptoms. But the same sort
of relief is likely to follow if the doctor prescribes a sedative drug or sugar pills, telling the patient that he will get
well. The effects of such suggestions as a rule prove transi-
tory; and even when the patient asserts that he has recovered, you probably can with care observe signs of nervous
irritability. Probably you soon find Mr. Doe again going
from doctor's office to doctor's office. Removal of his appendix and gall-bladder likewise fails to effect lasting
improvement, although for a time he feels somewhat better, following a long rest at the hospital.

Patients of this type are such frequent visitors at medical offices and hospitals that in extreme cases their incessant complaints finally tend to bore their doctors. Lack
of interest on the part of the doctor in the nervous and
mental complaints of the average patient, when no serious
pathology has been found, is likely to send that person
toward pseudoreligious cults and charlatanism. He seeks
relief in books on the "Power of Mind over Matter"; on
"New Thought"; on Psychology spelled with a capital P;
on theories that "Evil" and "Disease" do not exist; on the

cure of all diseases through manipulating joints or freeing nerves from imaginary pressure. In consequence, during recent decades the flow of coin has turned from the vendor of patent medicines in the direction of the cultists.

Many tense patients complain of symptoms which do not appear to them to have anything to do with the nervous system. Often the trouble seems to lie in some particular organ. One person has noted, for instance, frequent bowel movements with abdominal pain and perhaps with mucus in the stools for months or years. Another becomes constipated whenever he passes through trying situations. A third experiences a choking feeling in his throat, which interferes with his daily comfort and with his work and which is slightly relieved when he belches after taking soda. A fourth believes that he has heart disease since his heart sometimes beats very fast and hard and may even skip beats. Occasionally the complaint is frequent urination. Poor vision, in spite of a satisfactory report from the oculist, is not seldom mentioned.

Persons who have had some of the above-mentioned experiences often complain of so many different ailments that the physician pauses in perplexity and perhaps concludes that they must be due to neurosis. Of course, a thorough examination is in order.

We continue with the experiences of Mr. Doe. The story of the examination may run somewhat as follows: The doctor looks at Mr. Doe's scalp and hair and finds them practically normal. He shines a bright light on the pupils while Mr. Doe looks at a corner of the room, and they become small, as they do also when Mr. Doe looks at a pencil near by, which means that this test for syphilis of the nervous system is negative. The doctor looks into the nose and probably finds changes not considered important in the present connection. If infections appear in the teeth, Mr. Doe is referred to his dentist. The tongue may show a slightly grayish or yellowish coating. In excitable persons, examination of the tonsils and throat sometimes produces gagging. But touching the wall of the throat generally does not arouse any reaction in the condition technically known as "hysteria". While the patient swallows, the doctor's fingers glide over the neck; he finds that the thyroid gland is soft and of no unusual size and that there are no enlarged lymph glands. When Mr. Doe breathes deeply, his chest, let us assume, is seen to move freely in all its parts and maintains normal contour. The doctor now feels and taps the chest, outlining the heart and lungs. As he applies the stethoscope, he hears normal breath and heart sounds, aside from a quickened beat and perhaps a murmur, which he knows is not important.

After his patient lies down, his hand finds the liver and the spleen in proper position. If excited or fearful, the patient may be holding the abdominal muscles tense, interfering with the examiner's efforts to feel the contents of that region. In highly nervous persons, portions of the large intestine frequently are tender upon pressure and sometimes may be felt as a somewhat firm mass or a number of masses. Perhaps Mr. Doe has previously experienced a tenderness in the right lower portion of the abdomen, leading him to believe that he has chronic appendicitis. On this point the careful physician will not make a diagnosis until he has ascertained all the facts. Even if the appendix has been removed in recent years, there

may be tenderness in the region mentioned. The doctor
looks over the skin of the entire body and probably finds
nothing of note, except perhaps flushing. Using a rubber
tipped hammer, he lightly strikes certain tendons, including one below the knee, inducing a marked kick. These
tests disclose whether the muscle involved and the nerves
leading to the muscle are structurally intact. In many but
not all nervous persons the kick is relatively violent, showing that the local nerve and muscle tissues are tense. If
Mr. Doe is nervously excited during the examination, this
may cause a little fever, as indicated by the thermometer.
And if he is considerably worried about his blood pressure,
the doctor may find it increased. I have seen a rise of sixty
points in systolic pressure during such worry and a fall to
normal within half an hour as the patient became relaxed.
Accordingly, the diagnostician makes repeated readings
in order to ascertain whether the pressure is characteristically high. In chronically fatigued persons it often is somewhat low.

Mr. Doe is again sent to the laboratory. Specimens are
taken of his urine and blood. Perhaps he learns that they
prove negative, or possibly that the number of white blood
cells is above normal. This may indicate that he has an
area of inflammation somewhere, but in some instances it
means only that he was highly emotional at the time the
specimen was taken. Once more, he breathes into a tube
for half an hour, repeating the test of basal metabolism.
If he does not consume oxygen excessively, it indicates
that he does not have toxic goiter. Routine X-rays are
taken of his sinuses, teeth, heart and lungs. Let us assume
that they prove negative. After he has swallowed a glassful

of buttermilk containing barium, the doctor looks at the digestive organs. Wherever the barium appears, the X-rays cannot pass through, and so organs containing barium become clearly outlined. The X-rays are likely to disclose that the muscle walls of his digestive tract are contracted irregularly in various places, a condition commonly called "spastic".

Concerning the results of the examination, the doctor reports, "I agree with the physicians who have previously told you that there is no serious impairment in the structure of your nervous system or in other organs. But I cannot agree that there is nothing wrong with you and that your sufferings and inefficiency are imaginary. My observations disclose that as a rule too many of your muscles are contracting, not alone when you are busy but even also when you try to rest. This means that your nerves are overactive. You evidently are wasting energies in various directions with no good effect, and to this I would attribute the fatigue you complain of as well as your failure to secure sufficiently restful sleep. Furthermore, the X-ray examination definitely discloses that your digestive organs are overtense. My advice is that *you must learn to relax!*"

9

Overactive Nerves

"Overactive nerves" is the diagnosis following the doctor's examination of John Doe, and "overactive nerves" is the diagnosis on tens of thousands of other persons trying to adjust to the complexities and rush of modern life. Perhaps Mr. Doe is greatly interested and sees a light ahead; but he does not fully comprehend what is meant by the diagnosis or why the doctor believes that he must learn to relax. Consideration of his case leads to various interesting questions: What is happening in the nerves of persons leading excessively wearing lives or suffering from painful or distressing diseases? Is there anything which the research laboratory can offer to the doctor to give him a picture of what is going on? If so, the opportunity arises to substitute something definite for the guesswork and speculation that has been rife for decades in the field of "functional" and psychiatric disorders.

What is meant by "overactive nerves"? Before answering this, we recall that whenever you do anything, you contract muscles somewhere in your body. This applies equally to activities like breathing, which are essential to life, and to others, like talking, which often are better omitted. Every movement, then, depends for its occurrence upon the shortening of muscle fibers somewhere. Muscles compose about half of the weight of the entire body. Every muscle is supplied with a double set of nerves, one set bringing messages to the muscle, the other carrying messages from the muscle to the spinal cord and brain. Whenever the nerves coming to the muscle are active, the muscle which they supply is active. This activity in nerve and muscle is chemical in nature. It proceeds along a nerve like a wave, at a rate of about forty to one hundred yards per second in man. The wave is also electrical in nature, but as just indicated, does not pass so rapidly as does electricity along wires, which moves as fast as light.

From what has been said, it will be evident that when a muscle contracts, electrical waves are present not only in the muscle but also in the nerves that lead to and from the muscle. We can often get a better idea of our organism by comparing it with a machine. When an automobile is in motion, its wheels turn according to its speed. At sixty miles per hour, they revolve about thirty times per second. Rate per second also applies to nerves, for if measuring instruments are applied while a muscle fiber is contracting, they show that the discharge varies from about one to fifty per second. Certain recent tests suggest that the frequencies may be vastly higher. We can say, then, that "nerves are overactive" or that "nerve tension is high" if various nerves or muscles in the body are discharging more frequently than they normally should.

This is not the whole story. We have not yet said what frequencies are normal. Our knowledge on this point is not yet complete. In the case of blood pressure, we can state what is approximately the normal for any age, and if the figure for an individual is considerably higher, we say that he has "high blood pressure". Although the measurement is taken on the arm, it could just as well be taken on the leg or over any large artery conveniently placed, because the pressure in all of the large arteries at a given instant does not differ very greatly. But the nervous system is much more complicated than is the vascular system. The activity in one large nerve at any instant often differs in extent from that in another. As measured by the rate of discharge, one nerve may be found completely at rest while another shows great activity. It is this diversity in the nervous system which makes it difficult to arrive at an exact definition of "overactive nerves" or of "high nerve tension"—two terms which to us will mean the same.

Nevertheless, in practice and in the laboratory, we can generally tell whether nerves are overactive. We judge by clinical observations and by laboratory measurements, which will later be described. In much the same way we do not define what is meant by normal health; yet with the aid of clinical experience and laboratory tests, the physician generally is able to say whether the patient is well or ill.

Nerve discharge into muscle, then, produces muscular contractions, whereupon movements occur or else the muscle becomes more or less rigid. This gives us a convenient way to describe overactive nerves or high nerve tension. It is the failure of the individual to be relaxed when and where he should be normally.

An athlete running a race, a student writing an examination, a soldier at the front will naturally be in the state of high nerve tension. We should expect instruments attached to the muscles in action to record electrical discharges taking place at high frequency. But if the same individual lies down to rest and if no exciting conditions are present, we should not then anticipate that our instruments would record such discharges at high frequencies. Nevertheless, this is exactly what we frequently find in individuals who have been living overtense lives. Under conditions favorable to relaxation, recording devices show failure to relax. Nervous overactivity has become characteristic.

Can we be sure that persons who show nervous overactivity have not some disease, discovered or hidden? Many patients (and some doctors) are inclined to assume that where there is abnormal "nervousness", there must also be some "physical" cause. Their reasoning is generally confused, since they commonly speak of nervousness as not being physical, whereas we have just seen that it has very definite physical characteristics. However, what they really mean is that to cause nervousness there must be somewhere a tumor or an inflamed tissue or a disordered glandular secretion. The evidence that nervous overactivity does not necessarily arise from pathological disease rests first on the common finding of careful diagnosticians that many persons are neurotic, although frequent examinations disclose no important pathology; second, on the experience well known to all mankind that a succession of trying events or catastrophes obviously results in nervous irritability and excitement; third, on the relief from nervous symptoms of persons in whom definite pathology exists but is not removed, when difficulties in their lives are cleared up by changed circumstances or when they have learned to relax.

On the other hand, without doubt, almost any severe disease tends to contribute to the development of nerve-muscle overactivity. Most commonly this occurs when there is marked or persistent distress or pain. Almost everyone has had the experience of becoming increasingly tense during protracted headache, toothache or colic. I have frequently tested this matter on normal subjects resting quietly upon a couch in the laboratory, who previously have shown their ability to maintain relaxation. When a source of distress arose, such as headache or constriction due to a tight band used during an experiment, electrical currents were detected, indicating nerve-muscle overactivity.

Every physician has seen instances of nervousness arising from certain stimulating drugs or poisons taken by mouth. Such poisons also may be due to bacteria—for example, in certain stages of typhoid fever. Increased nervous activity is present during any condition of high fever and delirium; but it would be unwise to generalize from this that all bacterial infections, in all stages, are responsible for high nervous activity, because the matter has to be proved for each disease.

Owing to the distress and fear frequently associated with ailments requiring surgical treatment, patients often become increasingly nervous as the time for operation approaches. Following the operation, relief from the nervousness commonly occurs during a period of rest at the hospital. Both surgeon and patient should be cautious, however, in ascribing the nervous relief to the operation rather than to the enforced rest. In observing this caution, we do not minimize the importance of needed operations.

Occasionally patients relate that they have been nervous since an attack of food poisoning. They have vomited or had diarrhea. Unfortunately, we still lack tests for some types of food poisoning that probably exist. When a number of persons who have partaken of the same food fall sick at about the same time, the circumstantial evidence is clear. But when the patient suffers alone, has no fever, and perhaps shows marked nervous symptoms in other respects, the symptoms may have been due to a nervous upset. In the absence of decisive evidence, no conclusion should be drawn.

Nervous overactivity is present in the disease involving the thyroid gland, called toxic goiter. In this condition there is no doubt that excessive or disordered secretion from this gland causes high nerve tension.

After an acute infection, such as influenza, there sometimes follows insomnia or nervous irritability. Whether this consequence is due to the action of bacteria or to the distress and fretting about symptoms and confinement may be impossible to say.

Defects or disabilities which tend to make it hard for an individual to get along in his environment contribute to the development of nerve tension. Examples include poor vision or hearing, stuttering or stammering, crippled limbs, deformities and mental subnormalities.

Evidently, then, sources of pain and distress may cause nervous overactivity. Stimulating drugs and bacteria producing fever may have the same effect. Inflamed and swollen tissues, stretching the ends of sensory nerves, undoubtedly create high nerve tension. However, where pathology exists, like a chronically abscessed tooth or tonsil or other organ, but with no distress or pain, we must not assume that here likewise is a cause of increased nerve tension. For many persons have such conditions without being excessively tense, and the removal of such diseased areas is not followed in them by any noteworthy change in their nervous reactions. When tales are told of remarkable recoveries from insanity or marked nervous disorder after pulling a tooth which had not been painful, we should be very skeptical.

Many children become nervous because parents are overattentive. They become stimulated like the actor in the play who knows that his every movement is being watched. Overstimulation in the evening hours after the father has come home is particularly obvious.

Enough has been said to give a general idea of some of the causes of nervous overactivity. Many patients relate that their nervous symptoms arose apparently because of worries. Frequently the concern is over one's own health or that of some loved one, but commonly it is over money matters. How general are such experiences is shown by the amount of attention given to this theme in novels. In Henry Handel Richardson's *Ultima Thule*, for example, the chief character, having lost his fortune and his friends and finally a child by death, undergoes an apparently increasing nervous overactivity and gives a lurid description of his sufferings: "To wake in the night, and to know that, on this side of your waking, lies no ray of light or hope . . . only darkness and fear. To wake in the night: be wide awake in an instant, with all your faculties on edge:

to wake, and be under compulsion to set in, night for night, at the same point, knowing, from grim experience, that the demons awaiting you have each to be grappled with in turn, no single one of them left unthrown, before you can win through to the peace that is utter exhaustion. . . . The order in which his thoughts swept at him was always the same. The future . . . what of the future . . . ?"

Evidently the public is highly interested in the subjective phases of overactive nerves or high nerve tension and their causes. However, the chief purpose of the present volume is to disclose the objective phases and to discuss measures for their regulation or removal. We have concluded that nerves are overactive if they show evidence of electrical waves occurring at higher frequencies than they normally should. We note such evidence in anyone when his muscles are needlessly tense, whether during attempted rest or during activity. The causes of overactive nerves are various; but among these causes we particularly note the rush and complexities of modern living.

10

Tranquilizers

Quieting of nerves is often attempted through the use of medications known as tranquilizers. Their manufacture has become big business. This shows how widespread is tension among our populace. Tranquilizers alone are being sold at the rate of one hundred and fifty million per year and the public demand appears to be growing.

With the demonstration that even vicious monkeys could be rendered calm and manageable for a time by the administration of forms of "snake-root", the use of tranquilizing drugs was dramatically introduced into the daily practice of medicine. Today the demand has become so great that (where laws permit) druggists commonly dispense them to customers without prescriptions. Sometimes they are known as "happy pills".

Without doubt, there are times and places where tranquilizing agents can prove of use to many psychiatrists. They are being employed to advantage in state hospitals, especially on patients who are irrational and out of contact with nurses and attendants. They have been publicized extensively and are easy to prescribe and easy to take. Thus they constitute a temptation to the busy doctor, especially if he has little time or has little interest in more thorough methods.

Objections to the use of tranquilizers when unwarranted and excessive are growing in frequency. They are being voiced by many doctors.

Dr. H. A. Dickel and Dr. H. H. Dixon have pointed to the danger to the physician which results from accumulating pressure on the medical profession from the people who produce and those who demand these drugs. They apparently have in mind that fears and anxieties play a necessary role in the constructive efforts of any society and therefore should not be completely silenced by stupefying drugs.

Medical journals issue warnings in their editorial columns against the abuse of tranquilizers. In a letter addressed to the president of the Foundation for Scientific Relaxation, a distinguished editor states, "I heartily approve of any efforts to combat the current wholesale drugging of the public, which many of us view with considerable apprehension".

It is known that many of these medications excite side reactions or complications which include jaundice, skin eruptions, asthmatic attacks, blood changes and toxic delirium.

This has led to a search for tranquilizers with the least side reaction. Several have been found which satisfy this demand, more or less. However, even to these, individuals differ, some observing ill-effects. It is claimed that the best of them do not make the patient soporific, but many users get drowsy nevertheless. When under the influence at their work, their powers are lessened. Drive is reduced to such an extent that they have been called "don't-give-a-darn" tablets. Upon discontinuing certain tranquilizing medication, Dr. F. Lemere found that some of his patients felt nervous and let down.

Fortunately, there is more than one door open to the doctor who sets out earnestly to help the nervous, troubled, perhaps hypochondriac patient commonly seen in office practice. When he despairs of the pharmacological route, if he chooses, he can turn to physiological procedures which are direct and often no less effective. It has been shown that to calm the nervous, tense patient the doctor needs to understand the physiological measures which he employs no less than if he were employing medications. Thus he may be required to devote more time and study to the patient's needs than if he were merely to dash off a prescription. Reported results, however, suggest that often he may be well repaid for his efforts; and side reactions will not be encountered.

Physiological investigations make clear that tension states in man, including those which yield however partially to tranquilizing agents, always include temporary or lasting contraction in skeletal musculature. Furthermore, it has been learned that the skeletal muscular contraction reflects the purposes and efforts of the patient in meeting his problems, and in trying to achieve success in what he is doing. If he takes time for it, including a detailed history of the patient's tribulations and aspirations, the doctor can learn much about these states of tension-efforts in his patient. His next step is to acquaint himself with the physiology of progressive relaxation methods and to apply them however meagerly to his patient. He will find that the patient himself is endowed with what engineers might call a "built-in tranquilizer".

In considering the basic physiology, it is believed, he not alone comes to a better understanding of the tension-states which underlie his patient's symptoms; in addition, when he shows the patient that it is his own excessive efforts which are responsible for much stress and strain, he shows the way that leads directly toward relief. For we know that the tranquilizing drugs and indeed all sedatives produce their effect through toxic action on some portion of the brain-neuromuscular circuit, while physiological methods of progressive relaxation in no way disturb the circuit, but leave it intact. Not alone directness of approach and freedom from side-reactions would seem to favor the use of the physiological approach; but the evidence suggests that what the doctor teaches the patient as a way of living and of meeting his difficulties is likely to stay with him longer and produce more lasting effects than will any tranquilizer.

11

Quieting Your Nerves—Rest, Sedatives, Hobbies and Devices

Rest is nature's remedy for tension. This means that it is a good remedy; but this does not mean that it can not be bettered. The best means I know to better it are scientific relaxation methods. The results, I have found, are better than those produced by medicines, free from side-effects and more lasting. But especially in the hands of those not yet acquainted with these superior measures, there is a place for artificial rest induced by medicines.

We should be hasty, then, if we jumped to the conclusion that whatever is nature-given is perfect for all purposes of mankind. We know of countless examples where science has improved our lives. For example, nature has provided us with an inborn method of locomotion. This is by the use of our legs. We move freely as individuals even if only step by step. But science has added to this gift of nature other means of locomotion: automobiles, streetcars and railway systems, propeller planes and jet planes. To be sure, the materials employed are provided in the world around us; but the devices mentioned ensure speed and distance as our legs by themselves do not.

In a sense, "nature" produces living man himself and therefore indirectly whatever man produces. For those who prefer to think of "nature" in this wider sense as responsible even for the products of science, we must still distinguish between the locomotion provided by "nature" for primitive peoples, chiefly their legs, and our own scientific devices upon which much of our modern way of life depends.

Discussing rest, then, we distinguish between ordinary reclining to recuperate energies, with or without natural sleep (methods which primitive people enjoy), and scientific attempts to produce resting states.

Some of these scientific attempts have been made by chemists, and one such was discussed in the preceding chapter. Tranquilizers, we found, have a certain place in medicine but are being so widely employed as to threaten drive and achievement. Many doctors believe that they are an insidious public menace. The same applies to the promiscuous use of sedatives. This branch of big business is suffering a recession due to competition from tranquilizers; but nevertheless it is a national business of vast millions.

Physicians still frequently seek to quiet the nervous system not only by tranquilizers but also by sedatives. These include barbiturates, bromides and others. Both sedatives and tranquilizers commonly produce their effects by depressing nerve tissues. In using them, we should recognize that we are taking into our bodies substances which are toxic; in lay terms they act as very mild poison. By this action they temporarily depress and thus throw out of commission some portion of our effort-system.

Why should we thus depress ourselves when without resort to medicines we are capable of ceasing these same efforts? Surely a civilized people need not resort to "snake-root", barbiturates or other preparations to deaden efforts which result from their own initiative! A more direct and a healthier route lies open. Just as the shortest distance between two points is a straight line, so the shortest distance between making an effort and not doing so is direct scientific relaxation. Obviously this is an improvement on measures of self-depression by drugs.

Sedatives like bromides and barbiturates commonly produce a sort of dulling or deadening which more or less allays nervousness until another dose is needed. Long-continued use generally causes loss in effect, requiring increased dosage or change of medicines, and perhaps leads to dependence on the medicine. While sedatives doubtless are useful occasionally, particularly in certain acute conditions, many doctors, including the author, believe that they are now employed far too commonly.

Sedatives not only can prove habit forming but often depressing to the spirits in their after-effects. I have often seen such results. The patient may be emotionally disturbed in consequence, and his judgment about the difficulties which he faces may be discolored and even pathological. For these reasons alone many doctors prefer to employ them sparingly, or not at all.

Scientific relaxation starts (but does not end) as a development from practices of rest known to all peoples, however primitive, and to animals of all forms as well. In popular forms, rest is probably the remedy most generally prescribed by doctors in their daily practice. They advise rest, for example, in infectious fevers, in serious disorders of the digestive system or of the heart and blood vessels, in chronic tuberculosis, in chronic arthritis and in certain forms of goiter. Dr. William Osler wrote in 1910 that "the ordinary high-pressure business or professional man suffering from angina pectoris may find relief, or even cure, in the simple process of slowing the engines". In high-blood-pressure conditions, almost every doctor can tell of striking examples of reduction following protracted rest. Equally familiar are the ill-effects which so often follow a return to duties too soon after exhausting diseases such as influenza.

Many persons claim that they "relax" by driving, playing golf, collecting stamps or by some other hobby. What they mean by "relax" is vague in their minds; it certainly is not defined as in the present volume. When we have measured the nerve and muscular state of some of these persons at a moment when according to them they were relaxed, we have not confirmed their belief. They have been surprised at the moving lines shown on the screen indicating that they were tense indeed.

We do not find evidence for the common view that hobbies relax in our sense of the word. But we can agree that they often prove amusing and constitute worth-while occupations. What I am saying merely is that they do not have therapeutic value. For example, in a case of high blood pressure or of colitis, hobbies commonly fail whereas scientific relaxation generally accomplishes.

Massage and lukewarm baths are often prescribed in

order to induce rest or relaxation. As yet no accurate tests have been made which enable us to say to what extent they succeed. The same is true of golf and other sports, vacations and change of scene or occupation. Until such tests are made, we can draw no scientific conclusions about these various procedures. According to my clinical experience all such measures, while apparently highly useful for certain persons at certain times, nevertheless in many instances effect only moderate and temporary relief. Following a vacation or change of scene, as a rule, it soon becomes apparent that nervous tendencies have been abated but not cured. After the old life has been resumed for a time, the old habits and the old symptoms are likely to return.

All animals with nerves tend by various muscular movements to protect them from overstimulation. The frog generally raises his hind foot and wipes his abdomen if a little acid has been placed there to irritate his skin; he does the same more automatically if previously his brain has been removed. Evidently the action is regulated from the spinal cord. In daily life the ordinary man attempts through various means to prevent or to overcome nervous irritations by leaving or altering the environment he lives in, by attending to divers needs or ailments of his body, by taking in special foods or medicines, by altering his philosophy or motives or by listening to suggestion and persuasion.

He may leave or alter his environment, as by moving away or protecting himself from external sources of pain, loud noises, bright lights or other disturbances and from persons and situations that excite him; or by seeking a more satisfactory altitude or climate or room temperature. He may find relief in fresh air; he may try to destroy what troubles him; or, having suffered the loss of some object or person, he may endeavor to replace what he misses. Finally he may seek distraction from his cares in a hobby or in an adventure.

Attending to the body's needs and maladies often is effective in allaying particular nervous irritations. This may be attained when a person satisfies his hunger, thirst, sexual desires or the urges from bowels and bladder, as well as when he relieves restlessness by engaging in exercise. In certain diseases such as toxic goiter, nervous overactivity is allayed if the thyroid gland is partially removed. In general, massage, applying water to the body (hydrotherapy) and rest are time-honored customs in medicine to allay nervous irritability.

Food or medicine likewise can affect man's nervous activities. Some doctors advise their tense patients to avoid coffee and other forms of stimulating foods or drugs, possibly including spices, as well as meat and other proteins. The disease called beri-beri is marked by nervous symptoms, which are relieved by food containing vitamin B_1. This has led many doctors and pharmaceutical companies to recommend the use of this vitamin for common nervous conditions, including insomnia and colitis, although no proof has been furnished that these conditions are generally due to vitamin deficiency. In consequence of what has become almost a national fad, a considerable proportion of the patients who come to my clinic with nervous disorders relate that they have taken vitamin B, yet have much the same complaints.

A man's anxieties and worries can sometimes be diminished if he alters his ambitions or his outlook on life. Books on popular philosophy, the teachings of illustrious men like Epictetus, Epicurus and Marcus Aurelius are recommended by some physicians. The various religions tend to have influence in this same direction, particularly Buddhism.

Overemotional states frequently have been alleviated by argument, persuasion or suggestion on the part of friends or the psychiatrist.

Psychoanalysts believe that all nervous tension is fundamentally due to sexual maldevelopment during infantile years and can be relieved through measures leading the individual to become aware of these previously unconscious urges.

The various measures cited above to allay nervous irritation must be evaluated singly. Some are inborn, some are learned by the average person in daily life and some are the particular practices of groups of philosophers, religious teachers or physicians. When all is said and done, however, these measures have not proved adequate, in modern life at least, to prevent and remedy overactive nerves—as was sufficiently emphasized in Chapter 1. We therefore proceed to inquire what more you can do in this direction.

Even without learning to relax, there probably are ways for almost anyone who is living at too high tension to reduce it somewhat. To many, time taken out for rest seems a total loss. Adults, like children, prefer to keep going, even at bedtime, regardless of consequences. It is the function of the mind to protect the body and guard it for the future, but in this respect we seldom become quite mature. Time devoted to rest, like many another sacrifice in a good cause, is likely to reap an unexpected reward—in getting more things done per day than before.

Selecting the proper moment for rest has an importance not generally realized. If you are running for an entire day in a marathon race, eight quarter-hour rests distributed one each hour throughout the day will of course make you feel better than a single two-hour period of rest following the end of the race. During any sort of overexertion it is easy to observe that you get more tired each minute than you did at first; therefore, when greatly fatigued it is better to rest at once rather than wait until you have become completely exhausted.

Many persons can arrange for an hour of rest at noon. This period had better be before the meal for those with digestive disturbances; but for the average person the exact time does not matter. Businessmen and women who have no place to lie down at midday can generally find at least a comfortable chair to stretch out in with eyes closed. In the tropics and in various sections of Europe, the noonday rest formerly was a common practice. Prior to Hitler's epoch, even in Berlin a very busy physician closed his office at noon, retired to his home for food and complete rest before returning to work at two o'clock; and nobody wondered.

Another opportunity to interrupt the day's activities can generally be found before the evening meal. It is not necessary to remove any but uncomfortable outer garments. Rest in bed as a rule is more complete than rest in a chair and therefore is to be preferred, particularly for marked fatigue. Whether you lie down or sit up, however, the aim is as far as possible to cease contracting each and every muscle. When this is successfully done, you need not try to "make your mind a blank"; for, as will be seen later, complete muscular relaxation automatically shuts off mental activity, including worry.

"Get more hours of sleep" is probably good advice to the average city dweller. Amusement until a late hour, after a day of hard work, does not seem to be the best measure for health. Retiring at midnight readily becomes a habit hard to break; you can quickly learn to desire stimulating activities and to fight off natural tendencies toward sleep until they no longer occur as formerly. In my experience, the person who is tense (and therefore most in need of rest) *ipso facto* desires to continue to be active; while the individual who is relaxed is less likely to make such efforts.

Various additional measures can be found to aid the average person to economize in energy. Most persons fail to organize their daily affairs, permitting details and minor matters to occupy their attention overmuch.

Considerable energy is commonly wasted in unnecessary speech. Many who are given to this habit can do something toward diminishing it by reminding themselves many times each day. You should try to keep yourself from speaking, not by force but rather by letting the discussion drop. The aim is not to bother to say things unnecessarily, not even silently to yourself.

Obviously, comfortable chairs during business and social hours help you to keep relaxed. You are urged for a few days to keep track of the number of minutes in which you stand approximately still when you might as well be seated. Prolonged standing often results in greater subjective fatigue than does moderate exercise without bringing the same beneficial effects and should therefore generally be avoided.

Even without special training, you probably can do something to avoid undue irritability and excitement if you will frequently remind yourself to keep relaxed. Unfortunately, when something happens to excite you, you are likely to give your whole attention to the event, forgetting the cost to your nervous system.

While physicians do not encourage the practice of excessive attention to your own functions, there is a danger of going to the other extreme. A happy mean is reached when, not fearfully but with wise foresight, you note that you are beginning to get fatigued from any cause and cease the fatiguing activity as soon as is reasonably possible. You give heed to the feeling of fatigue because it is the signal that activity has been excessive. Obviously, the result is a saving of energy, which makes for health.

12

Scientific Relaxation

By relaxation in any muscle we mean the complete absence of all contractions. Limp and motionless, the muscle offers no resistance to stretching. For example, if your arm is completely relaxed, it can be bent or extended at the elbow by another person with scarcely more effort than is required to overcome the weight of your forearm; as if you were a rag doll, he encounters neither resistance nor aid when he moves your hand. In an individual lying completely relaxed, in the present sense, all the muscles attached to the bones are limp. These are called the "skeletal muscles". Whenever you make a voluntary movement, you do so by contracting some skeletal muscle or some group of skeletal muscles. General relaxation means the complete absence of all such movement. It means also the complete absence of holding any part of your body rigid.

When muscles are completely relaxed, the nerves to and from these muscles carry no messages; the nerves are completely inactive. From electrical tests later to be described, it is certain that relaxation in any set of nerves means simply zero activity in those nerves.

Most physicians and laymen as well as some scientific workers commonly use the word "nervousness". It seems safe to say that although the term is often used vaguely, it always means that nerves in some part or parts are active. Employing this usage, we can restate what was said above. *It is physically impossible to be nervous in any part of your body, if in that part you are completely relaxed.* The reader is urged to examine carefully the evidence and reasons for this statement as presented herein, and if possible also in the more technical volume, *Progressive Relaxation.* He is requested to consider whether this statement, if true, implies that in complete relaxation we have, to a certain extent, a direct and specific treatment for what is frequently called "nervousness".

During general relaxation, even certain involuntary movements are absent; for instance, if a sudden noise occurs, the relaxed person shows no start. But we are anticipating; let us, instead, return to our story.

Since physicians have found rest useful in the many and varied conditions enumerated in Chapter 11, it seemed important to seek by scientific means the most effective form of rest. This brought to attention the fact that the patient advised to remain in bed often fails to get the desired restful effects. He may not know how to relax, and his restlessness may be increased by distress of one kind or another; therefore he may shift and fidget in bed, lie stiffly or uncomfortably, owing to tense muscles; and may be worried, impatient or otherwise overactive in mind. In effect, the physician's purpose in prescribing rest in bed may be nullified. This doubtless explains the many failures which are commonly reported concerning the so-called rest-cure of Dr. Weir Mitchell. In 1879 this famous physician wrote a book entitled *Fat and Blood and How to Make Them*; he believed that diet was most important in the treatment of nervous conditions and assigned to rest a secondary place. Since then, some of his followers have emphasized rest more strongly.

Strange to relate, what occurs during rest has generally been so little studied that even in well-known treatises on nervous disorders the word "relaxation" seldom appeared until recent years. It has been less neglected by followers of certain cults. Annie Payson Call, a follower of Swedenborg, helped persons (1902) to cultivate poise and to use "relaxing exercises". Her work seems in certain practical respects highly commendable. But her interests are not scientific and when she states that an individual may remain nervous while relaxed by her measures, it is evident that she fails to study the extreme or finely drawn-out relaxation which is the essential aim of the present method.

In the course of laboratory studies presently to be described, a method to produce an extreme degree of nerve-muscle relaxation was gradually developed. What is customarily called "relaxation" was found in many instances to be inadequate and undependable for our purposes, both investigative and clinical. I found, as others had found previously, that an individual might lie on a couch apparently quiet for hours, yet remain sleepless and nervously restless. Even as he lay there, he might continue to betray signs of mental activity, organic excitement, anxiety or other emotional disturbance. He might breathe irregularly, fidget and start; might move his eyes, fingers or other parts of his body from time to time; or perhaps he might speak unnecessarily. These signs might occur occasionally or frequently and might either be quite obvious to the observer or require close inspection. When attention is once called to the matter, it is evident that such rest at best is not complete. Following it, the patient often fails to seem refreshed, retaining his symptoms and complaints of nervousness, fatigue or other ills. Accordingly, I was led to inquire whether the foregoing phenomena would not diminish or disappear if relaxation were cultivated in a greater degree and bodily extent.

It was evident that an extreme degree of relaxation was required, and for convenience I coined the term "progressive relaxation". The plan was to test whether excitement which has stubbornly persisted will tend under conditions favorable to progressive relaxation to give way to sleep, and whether spells of worry or rage or other emotional disturbance will tend to pass off. A further development aimed to produce a certain measure of these quieting effects even while the individual continued at work or other activity. In substance, the hypothesis was that a method could be evolved to quiet the nerve-muscle system, including what is commonly called the "mind".

When the unpracticed person lies on a couch, as quietly as he can, both external signs and tests generally reveal that the relaxation is not perfect. There remains what I shall call *residual tension*. This may also be inwardly observed through the muscle-sense. Years of observation on myself suggested, in 1910, that insomnia is always accompanied by a sense of residual tension and can always be overcome when one successfully ceases to contract the muscles even in this slight measure. Residual tension, accordingly, appears to be a fine, continued contraction of muscle along with slight movements or reflexes. Often it is reflexly excited, as by distress or pain; yet even under these conditions relaxation is to be sought.

Doing away with residual tension is, then, the essential feature of the present method. This does not generally happen in a moment, except with certain well-trained subjects, who are in practice. Frequently the tension only gradually disappears; it may take many minutes progressively to relax a single part of the body, such as the right arm. The desired relaxation may begin only when the individual might appear to an inexperienced observer to be very well relaxed.

Fatigued or nervous persons often fail to relax away residual tension. It is amazing how quietly such a one may appear to lie, while his arm or other part nevertheless reveals high nerve tension to the instrument used for recording this condition. Similarly, many persons who would not ordinarily be considered nervous or tense fail to relax completely.

When a person lies relaxed in the ordinary sense, but not completely relaxed in the physiological sense, the following signs reveal the presence of residual tension: his breathing is slightly irregular in time or force and perhaps he sighs occasionally; his pulse rate may be normal but is likely to be somewhat higher than that shown in later tests; the same is true of his temperature and blood pressure. If you watch him closely, you will see that he is not perfectly quiet, for he makes slight movements at times, wrinkles his forehead slightly, frowns, winks rapidly, contracts muscles about the eyes or moves the eyeballs under the closed lids, shifts his head, a limb or even a finger. The knee-jerk and other deep reflexes can be elicited (if there is no local nerve injury); he starts upon any sudden unexpected noise; in the studies undertaken up to date, if the esophagus or colon is spastic, it continues in this excited state. Finally, his mind continues to be active, and once started, worry or oppressive emotion will persist.

It is amazing what a faint degree of tension can be responsible for all this. The additional relaxation necessary to overcome residual tension is slight indeed. Yet this slight advance is precisely what is needed. Perhaps this again explains why the present method was long overlooked. As the individual relaxes past the stage of residual tension, his breathing loses the slight irregularities, the pulse rate may decline to normal, the temperature and blood pressure fall, the knee-jerk diminishes or disappears along with the throat and bending reflexes and the nervous start, the esophagus (assuming that the three instances studied are characteristic) relaxes in all its parts, and mental and emotional activity dwindle or disappear for brief periods. He then lies quietly with flaccid limbs and no trace of stiffness anywhere visible and with no reflex swallowing, while for the first time his eyelids become quite motionless and attain a peculiar toneless appearance. Tremor, if previously present, is diminished or absent, and slight shifts of the trunk or a limb or even a finger now cease to take place. Subjects independently agree in reporting that this resulting condition is pleasant and restful. If persistent, it becomes the most restful form of natural sleep. No university subject and no patient ever considered it a suggested or hypnoidal or trance state or anything but a perfectly natural condition. It is only the person who has merely read a description who might question this point.

High nerve tension, as shown in tenseness or exaggerated or excessive movements of the muscles which you move at will, presumably is subject to voluntary control. Every individual at least in some measure relaxes his muscles when he goes to rest. It would seem strange, therefore, if this natural function could not be specially cultivated to counteract an excess of activity and bring quiet to the nervous system. Such is the aim of the present method.

As may be readily noted, the overfatigued as well as the neurotic individual has partly lost the natural habit or ability to relax. Usually he does not know what muscles are tense, cannot judge accurately whether he is relaxed, does not clearly realize that he should relax and does not know how. These capacities must be cultivated or acquired anew. Accordingly, it is usually futile to tell the sufferer to relax or to have him take exercises to this end in gymnasiums. Following popular standards a patient may be apparently "relaxed" in bed for hours or days, yet be worried, fearful or otherwise excited. In this way at times the patient has been wrongly considered at rest, while voluntary or local reflex activities, as described above, have been overlooked. The detection of such signs is useful in diagnosis and in directing the patient or subject so as to bring about nervous and mental quiet.

According to my experience up to date in the clinic and in the laboratory, if the patient learns how to relax the voluntary system, there later tends to follow a similar quiescence of the viscera, including the heart, blood vessels and colon. Emotions tend to subside as he relaxes. To be sure, there may be a vicious circle: visceral nervous over-activity seems to stir up the central nervous system, where-upon this system stirs up the visceral system still more. The one system must become quiet before the other system can become quiet. So in certain chronic cases, relaxation becomes a gradual process—a matter of habit formation that may require months. Various stimuli that occur dur-ing pain, inflammation or disordered glandular secretion, such as toxic goiter, may give rise to visceral muscle spasm and therefore hinder relaxation. Under these difficult con-ditions, it is traditional to assume—and patients often assert—that an individual "cannot" relax. Yet such inability would be difficult to prove. The presence of a reflex re-sponse to pain or other stimulus, as will later be shown, is not in itself proof that the reflex "could not" have been relaxed. This is precisely what needs to be investigated, for the patient's subjective views as well as the physician's a priori conceptions should not take the place of laboratory and clinical tests.

For clarity, it seems worth-while to repeat what was said above, but in other words. Many persons ask, How is it possible to relax the stomach, the intestines, the heart or other internal organs? Can direct control be gained? The answer comes from experience in the clinical field as well as from laboratory tests, which indicate that if you relax your skeletal muscles sufficiently (those over which you have control), the internal muscles tend to relax likewise. You control the internal set to this extent, however in-directly, even without training. There is another way of

looking at it. The person whose visceral muscles are overtense, as presented in certain states of nervous indigestion,
spastic colon, palpitation and other common internal
symptoms, shows clearly to any qualified observer that his
external muscles also are overtense. Electrical measurements support this statement. If he relaxes the external
muscles sufficiently—those under his control—the symptoms from the excessive internal muscular tension subside,
while tests indicate that the internal muscles are no longer
so spastic. This suggests clearly that excessive tension or
spasticity in the visceral muscles depends more or less
upon the presence of excessive tension in the skeletal
muscles. If so, relaxation of skeletal muscles is effective in
the treatment of certain internal disorders because it
removes the cause, or an essential part of the cause.

After emphasizing the difference between "scientific"
and "ordinary" relaxation, it is equally important to emphasize their fundamental identity. Under favorable conditions untrained individuals relax, as shown by recording
instruments, although generally not so fully as after training. So-called phlegmatic individuals are particularly likely
to succeed. It may be assumed, however, that whatever
the natural propensities of an individual toward relaxation,
there is always considerably more that he can be taught;
just as anyone with a naturally good voice nevertheless
improves greatly with proper training. In my experience
persons who have not been trained to relax are less likely
at times of emotional disturbance to resort to voluntary
relaxation: they fail to apply the ability even if they have
it; yet the process of relaxation, whether natural or cultivated, is essentially the same.

Experience has shown that for the convalescent who is not confined to bed there is no conflict in prescribing exercise to alternate with rest. The one prepares for the other, and the degree and extent of relaxation are likely to be increased after moderate exercise.

Before training any patient, the doctor will of course take a detailed history and follow this with thorough physical, laboratory and X-ray examinations leading to a correct diagnosis. He may find it necessary to employ surgery or drugs or hygienic measures in addition to progressive relaxation. Obviously it is important to remove, as far as possible, both physical and mental sources of difficulty and excitement. Since this ideal often cannot be realized, the method of relaxation will seek to reduce the nervous reaction even when the sources remain unavoidably active.

If the purpose in employing relaxation is investigation rather than practical results, other measures of treatment must be excluded as far as possible. However, even considering only the practical interests of the patient, it is best in many instances to exclude additional measures of therapy until the effects of relaxation have been thoroughly tested; for otherwise, if the condition should become improved, doubt would arise as to what agent was responsible for the result, and in consequence the wrong one might be selected for continued use.

For the same reasons it is frequently best to have the patient follow his usual routine in his work and social affairs, learning to relax in the very presence of his difficulties. If his program is made lighter while he is trained to be relaxed, and he eventually recovers, there will be no way to determine how much benefit should be attributed to the relaxation alone, and he may give relaxation too much credit or too little. In the latter event he will neglect to practice after he is once well and may suffer a relapse.

The importance of daily practice cannot be too much emphasized to anyone who seriously intends to cultivate habits of relaxation whether lying down or during normal activities. Obviously neglect of practice may mean the loss of much that has been gained up to that point.

When the relaxation is limited to a particular muscle group or to a part of the body, such as a limb, it will be called *local*; when it includes practically the entire body, lying down, it will be called *general*.

We call the relaxation "progressive" in three respects: (1) The subject relaxes a group, for instance the muscles that bend the right arm, further and further each minute. (2) He learns one after the other to relax the principal muscle groups of his body. With each new group he simultaneously relaxes such parts as have received practice previously. (3) As he practices from day to day, according to my experience, he progresses toward a habit of repose— tends toward a state in which quiet is automatically maintained. In contrast with this, experience indicates that the individual who indulges in unrestrained excitement renders himself susceptible to further increase of excitement.

Evidently an important thing to learn about yourself is how you spend your energies. Such spending occurs when you contract a muscle. But often you stiffen a muscle or move somewhat without being aware of it, and in some persons such "unconscious" expenditures of energy are found in clinical practice to be frequent or habitual. This suggests the need for an inventory. The ability to observe your tensions obviously should aid you in the attempt to diminish certain ones. No fear need arise that such observation will lead you to become morbidly aware of yourself; rather, in my experience, it leads quite in the opposite direction.

When we say that a person is "tense", we mean, in popular terms, that he is "high-strung". When we say that a muscle is "tense", we mean that it is contracting; that is, its fibers are shortened. In addition, a third meaning of the term "tense" is used in this volume. If you will go into a quiet room, lie down and after a few minutes of rest make some movement slowly and steadily, you may, with practice, notice a sensation in the muscle which contracts. This experience we agree to call "tenseness". We agree also to call the same experience wherever it appears in the body and whatever its intensity by the same name. You are not expected to be a physician or physiologist when you learn to relax, and therefore are not expected to learn where your muscles are or what they are doing. But it is necessary for you to learn to recognize the sensation of tenseness. For this enables you to know when and where you are tense, in order that you may be able to correct the condition if excessive.

As previously said, muscle tensions make up much of the warp and woof of living. Walking, talking, breathing and all of our activities involve a series of complicated and finely shaded tensions of various muscles. To do away with all such tensions permanently would be to do away with living. This is not our purpose, but at times we need to control them, and relaxation is a form of such control.

Learning to recognize and locate your sensations of tenseness is helpful, but is not invariably needed, for relaxation often proceeds reflexly without your bothering about it; and this is always to be encouraged. If you watch your sensations and watch yourself relax continually or at a wrong moment, you will remain in a tense state. On the other hand, it is my common experience that some muscular regions frequently fail to relax completely until the subject learns to locate tenseness in them. A happy medium is reached when, with a minimum of attention, the disturbance is located and then relaxed. Moments of attention to muscles become increasingly unnecessary in the course of months as relaxation becomes habitual. This is like any other learning process, requiring less attention as time proceeds. After relaxation has been cultivated, it proceeds, at its best, automatically with little or no clearly conscious attention.

13

How to Relax Lying Down

To learn to pass from the state of tension that usually characterizes modern living into one of complete relaxation within a few minutes or less; to repeat this again and again until relaxation becomes habitual—such, from the present standpoint, are the aims of *nervous reeducation*.

This is a course which many persons will take weeks or months, perhaps years, to complete. It is not reasonable to expect to alter habits with the speed of taking a pill or buying a theater ticket. But the matter is not so difficult as it sounds. In fact, it is not difficult at all; rather, it is the easiest of things to learn. To clarify this matter, stretch out your arm and lift a heavy weight with it. As your muscles contract, you find yourself exerting effort; you find that the lifting is difficult. But suppose that you do not bother to lift the weight, just letting your muscles relax. This is the negative of exertion, the negative of difficulty. Nothing could be easier. But many persons have acquired habits of exerting themselves in everything they do, so that they contract some muscle or other even in trying to relax. In this way they make difficult what is not naturally so. We call this the "effort error".

Serious ailments, as previously said, are best referred to the physician, who decides whether relaxation or other methods are most fitting. The physician experienced in methods of relaxation observes and treats the patient for periods of about an hour, repeating them as often as seems necessary. If the patient is greatly fatigued, sleepless or excited but has not been so for longer than a few days or weeks, he may learn enough from a few treatments to be able to return approximately to the same state he was in before the onset of the acute disorder. But if the malady has persisted for years, it is not reasonable to expect quick results; the method of relaxation is not magic; it does not, like hypnosis and suggestion, seek to accomplish its effects overnight. In chronic conditions, the physician sees the patient twice a week or oftener, each time for about an hour, showing him how to recognize tensions and how to relax various parts of the body. After the patient has learned to be relaxed lying down, he is trained to relax while at work.

The patient practices by himself one or two hours each day. Practice is indispensable, just as it is in learning to drive an automobile, to dance or to speak a language. With the aid of instruction, he achieves his own recovery. This is why the physician who uses the method of relaxation does not depend for therapeutic results upon inducing the patient to believe that he will get well. Indeed, even to accept a statement from the patient regarding his recovery would not be scientific; the only way to be really certain that recovery has set in is through objective observations, including laboratory tests. In other words, both physician and patient may entertain a reasonable skepticism without interfering with the method, provided that instructions to relax are carried out conscientiously.

The person who wishes to find out what he can do for himself should seek a fairly quiet room. In order to prevent intrusion by adults and children, it may be necessary to lock the door. Interruptions from the ringing of the doorbell or telephone or from other sources should be averted. For each period of practice, as a rule, about an hour of seclusion is best.

A comfortable couch or bed should be selected, sufficiently wide for the arms to lie on either side without touching the body. Generally a pillow is used to support the head. This is not necessary for persons who prefer to do without, provided that the head does not fall back, straining the ligaments of the neck and producing fatigue. To prevent this, at least a thin cushion is needed as a rule. In order to avert pain in rheumatic individuals, thin cushions may be used also under the knees or under the small of the back.

The best position for the average person until he has become expert is flat on his back; that is, he faces the ceiling. The reason for not lying on one side or with chest down is that generally such positions involve strain in some part of the body. Each arm in its entire length rests directly on the couch in such a way that the hand is at least several inches from the leg. Folding the hands is avoided since it gives rise to sensations of contact in the skin that are likely to prove slightly disturbing. For the same reason, the legs are not crossed. Accordingly, each portion of the body is supported practically directly by the couch.

While these preliminary instructions should be followed by the beginner, it is well to emphasize that relaxation can be achieved in any ordinary position. Persons who are learning to relax while lying on the back need not hesitate to go to sleep in any other position to which they are accustomed.

Under the conditions stated, lie quietly on your back for about three or four minutes with eyes gradually closing. Delay in closing the eyes permits a more gradual letdown. You should neither speak nor be spoken to. After this preliminary rest, bend your left hand back at the wrist. While so doing, do not raise the left forearm, including the left elbow, from the couch, where it should rest throughout the period. This is illustrated in Fig. 1. While this bending is maintained and your eyes remain closed, you should observe carefully a certain faint sensation in the upper portion of the left forearm. To give yourself time to become acquainted with this faint sensation, continue to bend back steadily for several minutes. This sensation is the signal mark of tension everywhere in the body. It deserves your interest, for it can prove of daily help to you. Vague as it is, you can learn to recognize and to distinguish it from other sensations. This will enable you to know at any moment when and where you are tense.

Do not confuse this vague sensation which marks tension or tenseness with that other sensation which is at the wrist. When the hand is bent back at the wrist-joint, vague sensations arise in this joint which we call "strain".

Strain sensations are merely the passive results of your effort; they are more conspicuous as a rule than are sensations from muscle known as "tenseness", and often obscure these more important sensations.

Accordingly, the sensation experienced when a muscle contracts is to be called "tenseness". Note that this experience is dull or faint and is readily obscured. It differs in quality from the pain produced by pinching the muscle, from tickle, from touch produced by the application of cotton to the skin and from sensations of warmth or cold. If you scratch yourself with a pin or a pencil, you have an example of a sensation that is well outlined. But when a muscle is tense, the limits of the sensation are generally ill-defined, and the experience is diffuse. Tenseness, when moderate, is neither agreeable nor disagreeable but is particularly indistinct and characterless. To become familiar with the experience of tenseness so that it can be recognized wherever it occurs in any portion of the body is highly important in learning to relax.

During the first few periods we concern ourselves only with the left arm, neglecting tensions from other parts. In order for you to become familiar with the sensation of tenseness upon your bending your hand back, the action must be sustained. Be sure to bend steadily. Do not bend, then extend, then bend again irregularly. Such wavering motion or "seesawing" will fail to produce the steady sensation of tenseness which is desired in order to make you acquainted with the experience.

While observing the muscle-sense, you can observe better if you will keep your eyes closed. (People often close their eyes thus in order to note some delicate experience,

such as a faint fragrance.) You will not need to learn
where your muscles are located, nor should you feel them
with your fingers when they tighten during contraction.

Some persons are slow in the cultivation of the muscle-
sense. They generally are retarded in gaining the fine
control of relaxation which comes to those who learn to
recognize their muscle sensations. But even without this
ability, a fair if not a complete measure of relaxation may
be attained. It pays to be patient, to try again and again
to recognize these sensations. For on the second or third
day you may be able to note readily what seemed extremely vague and doubtful at first.

When you are satisfied that you clearly perceive the
sensation of tenseness upon bending the hand back, you
may realize, "This is you doing! What we wish is simply
the reverse of this, namely, *not* doing!" Thereupon you are
to discontinue bending the hand back, which should permit the hand to fall by its own weight. You can notice
that the sensation called "tenseness" diminished or disappeared from the forearm region. It is agreed to call the
disappearance or absence of this sensation "relaxation".
We have defined the chief words, which we are to use,
in terms of your experience.

As you relax the muscles that have bent your hand, you
begin to learn clearly what it is *not to do*. You begin to
realize that relaxation is not subjectively a positive something, *but simply a negative*. After you have relaxed your
arm for several minutes to illustrate this point, bend back
the hand once more and then relax again. This time you
are to observe that the relaxation involves no effort: you
did not have to contract your arm, or any other part in

order to relax your forearm. These are important points to learn, for the untrained individual who fails to relax will contract various muscles in a vain effort to succeed. Make certain that you do not pull your hand down to the couch with a jerk when you let go; also that you do not move it slightly after it has reached the couch in order to make it comfortable. Such motions are often made by the beginner, who believes that he is relaxing; but they are unnecessary and definitely are contrary to methods of relaxation.

Bending your hand back again, you note that this is *effort*. But ceasing to bend your arm, relaxing it properly, involves no effort. It is important to realize that relaxation never is "hard" and cannot be; it is either done or not done, and that is all.

When these matters have been understood, bend back the hand again and let it go. Upon discontinuing this act completely, the hand should fall limply. Do not actively move it back to its former position. Lowering the hand instead of letting it fall limply is a mistake made by many.

As you will readily understand, bending the arm is *not* a "relaxation exercise". Bending at the wrist or any other act does not produce relaxation. The acts illustrated in the figures are performed solely in order to create examples of what you are not to do when you relax. Contraction does not increase the relaxation present before the contraction. Physical exercise is the opposite of relaxation. It is doing something muscular, a positive act. Relaxation (going negative) is the reverse.

Following these preliminary attempts to recognize the sensation of tenseness, permit yourself about half an hour for continuous relaxation. *Do not continue to contract from time to time during the period,* or you will destroy the benefits from this relaxation. After contracting several times as directed, you are to devote the entire remainder of the hour to complete rest, avoiding any movement whatsoever, yet not "holding yourself still".

After you have recognized contraction in a muscle group, you can practice relaxing it completely. You are to learn to recognize contraction in the various parts of your body in a certain order. The large muscles are studied first, because the sensation therefrom is most conspicuous. As you relax a given part, you *simultaneously* relax all parts that have received practice previously.

On the following day it is well to have a second period of self-instruction. As previously, your arms are to rest beside you, not in contact with your clothes. Begin by letting yourself become limp on the couch in order to prepare yourself to recognize faint muscular sensations, which otherwise might be obscured by other sensations. After about ten minutes of rest with eyelids open at first but closed later, bend your left hand back as you did the day before (Fig. 1), noting the sensation in the muscles in the upper portion of the left forearm. Then discontinue bending, letting the muscle rest completely for several minutes. Following this review of yesterday's practice, bend the left hand forward at the wrist as shown in Fig. 2. Continue to bend steadily while you try to locate the feeling of tenseness. It may elude you at first, but continue to try to observe it. Do not seesaw, but maintain the tension steadily. Eventually you should find it in the lower portion of the left forearm, as shown by the arrow in Fig. 2.

But give yourself a chance to find it before you look for the location shown by the arrow.

Be sure to distinguish the sensation of tenseness thus recognized from the sensation of strain in the wrist.

Having observed the sensation during about one minute of steady bending, cease to bend. Go negative. This means what it says: do not make any effort to restore your hand to its former position. Such an effort would not be relaxing, but would be tensing. Any effort to relax is failure to relax.

You are to bend your hand forward three times (no more) during this hour of practice on the second day. The bending should be maintained without seesaw for about one minute for observation time. Between each act of bending, allow an interval of about three minutes during which you are to remain relaxed in the forearm.

After the third (final) bending, the forearm (and the remainder of you) is to remain relaxed for the remainder of the period. Accordingly you are to avoid bending again, letting your muscles relax as completely as you know how during the final half-hour of the practice period.

Instructions for the third period are most simple. Begin as previously, lying on your back with eyes open for several minutes; then let the eyes close gradually and do not reopen them, because no tension is to be performed. Your aim will be to maintain relaxation in the left arm— nothing more. This will require you to note the onset of tenseness, should this occur at any moment in the left upper arm. If it begins, you may be able to detect it, however slight and invisible, and to relax it, for it is *you* doing something. You are responsible for any shifting that arises, and, whatever your excuses, you are to avoid it. Simple as are the instructions, you will be entitled to a good mark if you carry them out successfully.

In the fourth period, begin as you did on the previous occasions. After your eyelids have been closed for a brief interval, repeat the movements performed in the first and second periods. That is, bend the left hand back at the wrist for about one minute, observing carefully once more the sensation from tenseness in the upper portion of the left forearm, in contrast with the strain at the wrist and also the strain in the lower portion of the left forearm which you may now discern. Having done so, go negative. The hand should drop limply and relaxation should be maintained for several minutes. Thereafter bend the left hand forward at the wrist, observing as you do so the sensation from tenseness in the lower portion of the left forearm, in contrast with strain at the wrist and also the strain in the lower portion of the left forearm which now may have come above the horizon of your perception. Having observed thus, go negative for several minutes.

In following the directions given in this book, do not attempt to be precise in timing your acts of tensing or the periods of relaxation. When you are to bend back your hand for about one minute or are to relax thereafter for several minutes, do not perform by the clock or your wrist watch. It is better to estimate the time, for there is no need to be accurate in this.

Another precaution: Do not review more than three acts of tension in any hour of your practice. If you continue to tense one part after another (as many have done wrongly), you will fail to learn to relax because your hour will be devoted instead chiefly to physical exercises.

After the preliminary review, you are ready to begin your new task of the day. As shown in Fig. 3, bend your left arm at the elbow (to an angle of about thirty degrees), letting the hand drop limply at the wrist. In doing so, take care not to raise the left elbow from the couch. Remember to keep your eyelids closed during the entire hour of practice, except only during the beginning few minutes.

While bending the left arm at the elbow, look for the faint sensation of tenseness in the front part of the upper arm (where the biceps muscle is located).

If you are having difficulty in recognizing tenseness, the reason probably is that you are looking for too much. The sensation is delicate and you should adapt yourself to this fact. Do not look for a striking sensation, like pain or even like strain. If you wish, you may ask someone to hold back the forearm while you are bending at the elbow. This will intensify the sensation from the biceps region. But prepare yourself to discern sensations from muscular regions in the future without similar measures of reinforcement.

After discerning or failing to discern the sensation from tenseness during the act of bending for about two or three minutes, go negative. The forearm, including the hand, should fall limply as if this portion of you were a rag doll. Maintain the negativity for about three minutes. Then bend at the elbow once more for about one minute to allow for observation, after which go negative for several minutes. Thereafter bend at the elbow a third and final time for about one minute to allow for observation once more, after which go negative and remain so during the final half-hour.

In the fifth period (on the fifth day), follow the procedure illustrated in Fig. 4. Your wrist is to rest on one or two books in thickness about four inches or a little more. The books may remain in place throughout the hour. You may omit the review of tensions observed in preceding periods.

In this period, begin as usual with eyes open but closing gradually. Once more, be sure to keep the eyes closed thereafter during the entire hour period. After the eyes have been closed for several minutes, press the wrist gently against the books, while noting the sensation from tenseness now in the under surface (the back part) of the upper arm. Do not be confused by the strain in the fore-part or in the elbow.

Following the order of procedure employed previously, observe the sensation from tenseness (for several minutes or less) three times in all. Go negative each time following the observation. Devote the last half of the period (like all other periods) solely to relaxing. This means that you are then to omit all movements whatsoever.

Period six, like period three, is to be devoted from the very outset to relaxation alone, omitting all deliberate tensions.

By the seventh period you may have become familiar with the sensations from the chief muscles of the left arm. Now is the time for you to experience that a part need not be moved in order to become progressively relaxed. While your arm continues in contact with the couch, stiffen the muscles so that the entire arm becomes rigid, but do not move it in any direction. Begin by making these muscles a little stiff and gradually increase more and more for about thirty seconds. After reaching a maximum do not contract quite so much as before, then a little less, still less, and so on and on, past the point where the arm seems perfectly relaxed, and even further. This is what is meant by "going in the negative direction". Here, then, is the type form of progressive relaxation for all subsequent periods. Whenever in the early stages of practice you believe that you have completely relaxed some part of your body, you may safely assume that you are mistaken and that the part is at least slightly tense. Some degree of residual tension probably still remains, and your task is to do away with this entirely. Therefore, after you have ceased to hold your arm rigid until the point has been reached beyond which you seem unable to go, *whatever it is that you have been doing up to this point, continue that on and on.* This may give you the concrete experience of progressive relaxation in an arm.

The warning is here repeated that one part of the above-mentioned illustration is not to be followed in the future: as a rule you should not stiffen the arm or engage in some other contraction before you relax, but should begin to relax at whatever stage you find yourself. Graphic records have revealed that subjects sometimes fail to reach extreme relaxation because they contract at the moment they try to relax. If it is poor practice to contract every time before you relax, evidently steps should be taken toward preventing this from becoming a habit. Accordingly, not alone are you to omit all tensions in practice periods number three and six, but similarly in periods number nine, twelve, fifteen and subsequent multiples of three.

Another warning of great importance is that you should not try to aid relaxation by repeating such sentences as

"Now my arms are becoming numb!" or "My limbs are feeling heavy!" or "This is doing me good!" You are not to give yourself suggestions but are only to learn to relax just as you might learn to dance or swim.

If you have met with fair success in recognizing tensions, you may at the seventh period or somewhat later be made familiar with what I shall for brevity call *diminishing tensions*. You bend your arm, as shown in Fig. 3, noting the sensation of tenseness in the biceps. The bending is repeated halfway, then half of this and so on. A point is soon reached at which you are to bend it so slightly that an onlooker could scarcely note the movement. If you are still able to note the tension, you are to bend it again, but a little less, so that no movement would be outwardly discernible. Patients report (and electrical measurements confirm) that the experience of muscular contraction is again repeated but is considerably fainter than before. If you seem to confirm this finding, you are to bend again but still less than before. After several diminutions from this stage, the experience vanishes.

No one can learn to control his relaxation who does not know the difference between what we call "tenseness" and "strain". This test arises, for instance, when you bend your left hand backward in an attempt to locate the sensation called "tenseness". A common mistake is for you to point to the top of the wrist, where a tightness or pressure attracts attention, and to fail altogether to note the fainter sensation of tenseness which is in the upper portion of the forearm (see Fig. 1). If you make this mistake, you are requested to keep the left hand relaxed at the wrist while someone bends it back. You can then note the same tight-

1 While you bend your hand backward, you observe *tenseness* in the back part of the forearm.

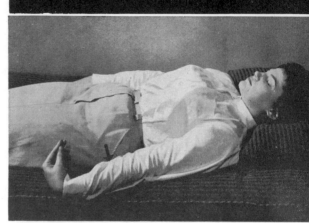

2 While you bend your hand forward, you observe *tenseness* in the front part of the forearm.

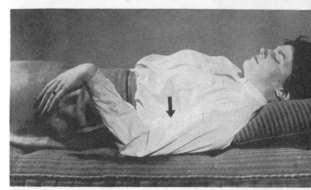

3 Closing your eyes, bend your left arm steadily. You are to notice the sensation in the flexor muscles where the arrow points, which is called *tenseness*.

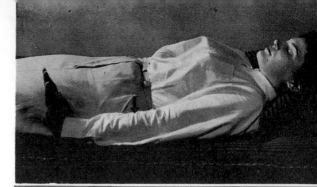

4 As you extend your arm, pressing your wrist down against the stack of books (while your hand remains limp), you become familiar with *tenseness* in the extensor muscles, where the arrow points.

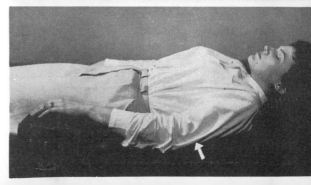

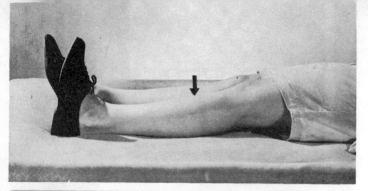

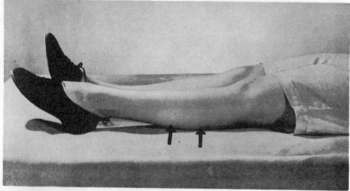

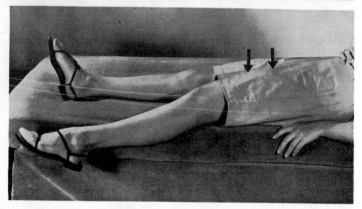

5 Bending your foot up, you observe *tenseness* in the muscles below the kneecap.

6 Bending your foot down, you observe *tenseness* in the muscles of the calf.

7 Extending your leg, you observe *tenseness* in the front part of the thigh. (Previously, while relaxing, with your leg over the edge of the couch, your shoe was nearer the floor.)

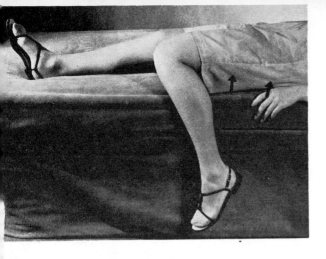

❧ Bending your leg (raising your foot backward), you observe *tenseness* in the back part of the thigh.

9 Bending at the hip, with your left leg hanging limply over the edge of the couch, you should localize *tenseness* in the flexor (psoas) muscles, which are located deep in your abdomen toward your back.

10 Pressing the lower portion of your thigh down against the stack of books, you produce *tenseness* in the muscles of the buttock.

14 Bending the head directly to one side permits you to observe *tenseness* in the neck on that side.

11 Drawing in the abdominal muscles, you observe faint *tenseness* all over the abdomen.

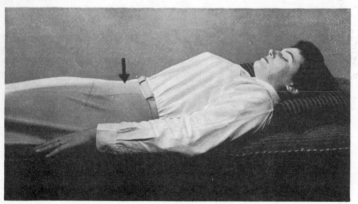

12 Arching the back, you should observe marked *tenseness* along both sides of the spine.

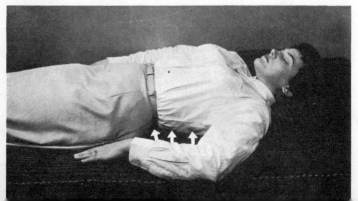

13 As you inhale deeply, you can note very faint and diffuse *tenseness* all over the chest.

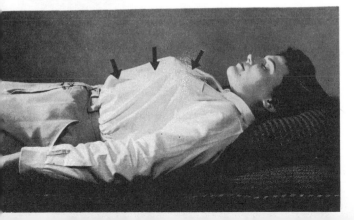

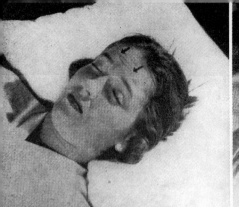

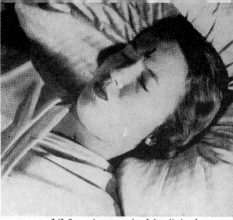

15 Wrinkling your forehead is the occasion of *tenseness* diffusely over your entire forehead.

16 Frowning can be felt distinctly in the region between the eyes.

19 Looking from ceiling to floor, you should report that you see the ceiling and then the floor, and that you observe *tension* in the eyeballs in doing so. This *tension* changes rapidly as the eye moves, and for brevity is called a *moving tension* to contrast it with the fairly *steady tension* you experience when a muscle is held rigid as in Fig. 1.

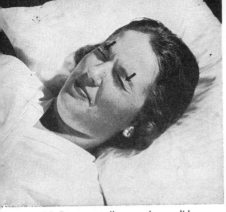

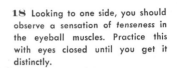
18 Looking to one side, you should observe a sensation of *tenseness* in the eyeball muscles. Practice this with eyes closed until you get it distinctly.

17 *Tenseness* all over the eyelids can be observed upon closing them tightly.

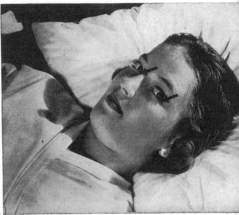

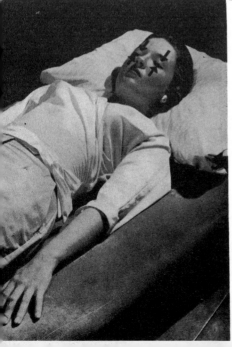

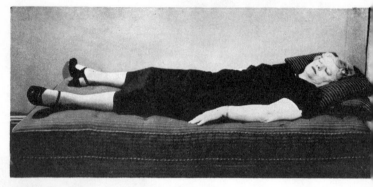

20 This illustrates complete *general relaxation*.

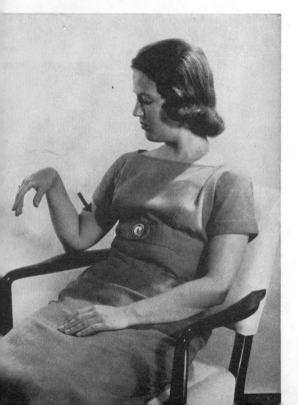

21 In the sitting posture, you are to review all the *tensions* previously performed lying down. Bending the arm, you should be able to feel the *tenseness* very clearly.

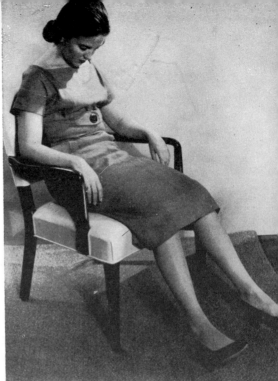

22 This illustrates how relaxed a person can be while sitting up. It is called *differential relaxation*.

23 Another example of *differential relaxation*. This lady is learning to relax so far as is possible while reading a book and getting the meaning.

25 In the present studies, tension has become a measurable reality (replacing the vague use of this term commonly employed). Here is a young doctor learning to be relaxed as he sits at a desk. He is helped when he can see on the visioscreen just how tense he is at any moment in his forearm muscles. Platinum-iridium electrodes lie on his skin above these muscles. From these electrodes, wires pass to recording instruments developed in our laboratory.

24 At work, but *differentially relaxed*. She is saving her energy and is more efficient.

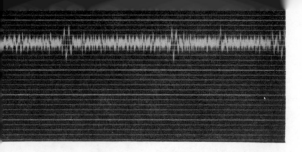

26 During complete relaxation of a muscle being tested electrically, the shadow of the recording wire is practically quiet. As the photographic film moves (left to right), the only variations seen are slight constant ones (arising in the instrument) and pulse beats (four shown here).

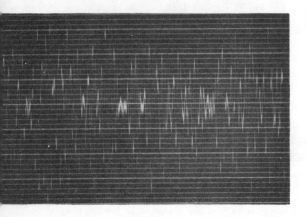

27 Tenseness in the muscle is disclosed here. Marked vibrations of the shadow produce these long approximately vertical lines, the length of which depends upon the voltages in the muscle. These voltages vary with the degree in which it is contracting. Thus we are now able to measure electrically, with the aid of a moving picture, activity or relaxation in human nerve or muscle. After the record shown in Fig. 26 was taken, the subject continued to lia apparently motionless; but she became tense, as shown by frequent movements of the wire-shadow. These movements were so great that it was necessary to turn a dial, rendering the instrument about one-tenth as sensitive, in order to register the full length of the vertical lines on the photograph. At full sensitivity, each milli-meter of length in a vertical line indicates about three-millionths of a volt.

ness or pressure at the wrist as previously, when you were bending your hand backward. If observant, you will decide that these sensations at the wrist are by no means the same as the experience which it was agreed to call "tenseness". They are more definite in character than "tenseness", are more clearly outlined and, in general, feel different, just as warm differs in feeling from cold, tickle from touch, or pain from the other sensations mentioned. Accordingly, it is important to distinguish the sort of sensations noted at the wrist by another name, such as "strain". While your hand is bent backward without effort on your part, try to relax the strain at the wrist. You will fail, for the strain is not you *doing*, although it is often present and under favorable circumstances may disappear when you relax. If, while your hand continues to be bent backward by your assistant, you bend it backward still further by an additional effort of your own, "tenseness" now makes its appearance on the top of your forearm, whereupon the distinction should become apparent. When you relax your hand, the "tenseness" gives way to relaxation, but the strain at the wrist continues while your assistant bends back the hand.

In this manner you discover that sensations of tenseness are readily overlooked because of their relative faintness. These sensations are sometimes "unconscious" in the sense that they are commonly overlooked. Without doubt, in this sense, "unconscious" experiences can be relaxed away.

Another distinction to be learned is between experiences of *moving* and *steady* tensions, that is, changing muscular contractions versus rigid states. Flexion of the arm is an

instance of a moving tension, while holding it rigid illustrates a steady tension.

Other muscle groups should receive practice in the preceding manner with variations according to your particular needs. Practice is devoted to the right arm in the same
manner as described above for the left. After about twelve
periods you may have completed both arms, but it would
doubtless be better to spend about twenty or thirty periods
up to this point. When you have learned to recognize
tenseness in any muscle group, for instance the biceps, it
is well to permit a few days to elapse, during which your
daily practice concerns only this muscle group, while from
time to time as you go about your affairs you bend your
arm for an instant, noting the sensation and localizing it.
This will require very little loss of time from other matters,
but you will have the benefit of many repetitions. As in
seeing a particular face over and over again, you gradually
become very familiar with the experience of tension in a
particular region and can recognize even its faint forms
with a minimum of effort and attention.

You are to learn to recognize tension in six muscle
groups in each leg: Bending the foot or toes toward your
face causes tenseness, not at the ankle or instep but in the
front of the leg somewhat below the knee (Fig. 5). Bending the toes or foot down gives tenseness, not near the
ankle but in the calf (Fig. 6). The experience of tension in
the thigh can be brought out clearly if, during periods six-
teen and seventeen, you lie in such a way that your left leg
hangs limply over the side of the couch throughout the
hour except when you perform the tensions. If the couch
(or bed) is fairly high, your foot will not reach the floor.

Extending (straightening the leg) should be performed as in Fig. 7, with the foot limp at the ankle joint. Your tendency will be to hold it rigid there. Maintain the posture shown in the figure until you clearly recognize the sensation of tenseness in the front part of the thigh. Bending the left leg as shown in Fig. 8 arouses the sensation in the rear part of the thigh. Bending the thigh upward arouses sensations deep in the abdomen in the hip region (Fig. 9); in order to bring out the experience the leg should be relaxed at the knee, so that the heel moves limply along the couch as the thigh bends. Extending the thigh downward against a stack of books on the couch arouses sensations of tenseness as high up as the region of the buttock, where patients frequently overlook it (Fig. 10).

If at this or at any other stage, aiming to relax seems difficult or "trying", you may be certain that this is because you are contracting somewhere. Probably you are making the "beginner's error", that is, making an effort to relax. On the other hand, it is a sign of progress when you begin to enjoy giving yourself over to rest.

Subjects often report that complete relaxation is accompanied by no particular conscious feeling at all. Rather, they say, various sensations seem to fall away from a part as it becomes fully relaxed. One reports, "After a period of time I am no longer aware where my arms lie with regard to my body. The sense of location has lapsed."

On the other hand, if upon practice you feel "as if separated from your body" or have any strange sensations at all, pleasant or unpleasant, you are not relaxing as here taught. You had better stop altogether for the time being and begin again another day.

We pass now to the trunk. You are to draw in the abdominal muscles, producing a diffuse experience of tenseness, readily noted over the entire front of the abdomen (Fig. 11). The same experience arises there if, after you have been reclining on your back, you bend up and forward. Bending backward (arching the back, Fig. 12) is accompanied by tenseness along the spine on either side. You should relax for a half-hour before you try to localize tenseness in the muscles of breathing (Fig. 13). Upon taking a deep breath, a faint diffuse sensation occurs all over the chest wall while you breathe in, but not markedly while you breathe out. Patients sometimes wrongly state that they experience the tenseness in deep breathing solely under the chest bone and solely for the period when the breath is held. After you have succeeded in recognizing tension during deep breathing, you have the opportunity to notice it during ordinary breathing. The way to relax your chest is precisely as you relax your arm—letting the breathing go by itself. "Controlled breathing" is not used as an aid to relaxation in the present method. Rather, the aim is to free the respiration from voluntary influence.

Various cults and various religious practices of the Orient, including Yoga, make a feature of "breath control". The practices mentioned are mystical or religious rather than scientific and in my opinion are to be avoided by persons who consider their health first. In many instances they include hypnotic or hypnoidal states. However sincere the practitioner, a psychological understanding of what is performed is generally lacking. Suggestions and autosuggestions are given without clear realization of the fact. There can result injury to the personality, particularly the autonomous regulation of energies, to which this volume is dedicated.

After practicing relaxation of the breathing muscles, you come to the shoulders. In connection with each shoulder, recognizing tensions is of importance in three regions. Extending the arm forward and inward is accompanied by tenseness in the front part of the chest adjacent to the arm. Moving the shoulders backward and toward the spine is accompanied by tenseness between the shoulder blades. Shrugging the shoulders is accompanied by tenseness at the top of the shoulders and in the sides of the neck.

To become acquainted with tensions in the neck, you incline the head to the left (Fig. 14), to the right, forward, and backward, noting tenseness respectively (chiefly) in the left side of the neck, in the right side, in the front and both sides, and in the back of the neck. After each location has been recognized at the beginning of a period of practice, the remainder of the period is devoted to ceasing to make that contraction even in the slightest degree—"letting the head fall limply, like a rubber ball".

RELAXING THE EYES

The ability to relax the eyes, including the brow and lids, is a crucial test of skill. It is easy for most persons to distinguish tenseness in wrinkling the forehead (Fig. 15). The experience is located beneath the wrinkling skin. This region is then permitted to flatten out. Patients sometimes report that they can distinguish the sensations as they diminish for periods of many minutes. After frowning (Fig. 16), the brow likewise is gradually unfurrowed. You must take care that you do not wrinkle your forehead in trying to smooth your brow. If you make this mistake, you must try again, for you should learn that *it is not necessary to move in order to relax*. Next in order, the lids of the closed eyes are shut tightly, and tenseness is noted in the lids (Fig. 17). Gradually let the lids go, until winking of the closed lids has become infrequent or absent. At the next period look to the left with eyelids closed and note the tenseness in the eyeball region (Fig. 18). Observe again, looking to the right, later up and down. Look straight forward, noting the static tension in the eyeball region. Each movement or act is repeated until the experience is clearly discerned. Then let the eyes go completely, *just as you let the arm go.* You are not to try to look in any direction. If you fail to relax the eyeballs, stiffen your right arm and then gradually let your arm and eyes relax together. As a rule many repetitions are needed.

After a fair measure of success, open the eyes. Observe what takes place in the region of your eyes as you look from ceiling toward the floor and back. You will experience a transient sensation of tenseness. Repeat several times so as to bring the experience to your attention vividly. You are using the eyes to look, and the sensation of tension can be a direct indication to you (if you learn to observe it) of the slight expenditures of energy involved.

There is more than one reason for your interest in this. In the past you have used your eyes with no awareness of how much at any time. If you would avoid overuse of the eyes, a first step is to become acquainted with means to recognize the muscular tension present whenever they are used, whether much or however slightly. In following the objectives and the directions of this book, you are seeking to save yourself from unnecessary use of your energies, in order to reserve those energies for things most worthwhile in life. In this objective, the eyes deserve special consideration; for they trigger the expenditure of energies over your entire body. This is because what you see (or imagine you see) determines largely what you do.

Try to become familiar, then, with the tension present in eye motion. Note also the *steady tension* present when you look at a fixed point in front of you perhaps five to ten feet away. Distinguish the sensation of tenseness from the sensations from burning and from strain. These sensations are more readily recognized, but they only result from activity; they are passive, like a broken arm. Tension is more important, for it is *you* doing.

Whenever you are in doubt what tension should mean to you, whether in the eyes or any other region, bend back your hand at the wrist. Thereupon notice once more the sensation in the upper section of the forearm which we know as tension. This will keep the experience fresh.

RELAXING MENTAL ACTIVITIES

Many persons complain that "the mind keeps on working" after they lie down to relax, preventing sleep. Some even inquire in advance whether muscular relaxation will quiet the mind. The answer to these complaints or queries is for you to find from your own observations. Thus prejudice is avoided. *At no time should you make an effort to stop thinking or to "make your mind a blank". Throughout the course your sole purpose is to relax muscles progressively, letting other effects come as they may.*

For the following matters you will need a particularly

quiet room, free from even such slight disturbances as the sounds of footsteps or of rustling papers. After about fifteen minutes of complete or almost complete relaxation of all the regions which have so far received practice, with eyelids closed, you are to imagine that you see the ceiling and then the floor of the room in which you are lying. If you succeed, you may note sensations of tenseness about the eyeballs like those which you experienced previously when with open eyes you looked from the ceiling to the floor. These sensations are sometimes readily recognized but in many instances they are so slight that frequent repetition is required. After engaging in imagination as above indicated, you are to relax your eyes completely for five to fifteen minutes. Next you are to imagine seeing the wall on your left side and thereafter the wall on your right, making your observation. Practice imagining each wall successively until you become skilled in observing the tensions present when you imagine. Upon relaxing your eyes, visualization ceases.

At the next period of your practice you will again allow a preliminary interval for becoming relaxed. Thereafter you are to imagine a motorcar passing. If you are quick enough at observation, you will probably note a flashlike visual picture of a motorcar accompanied by a slight sensation of tenseness in the region of the eyeballs, as if the eyes are turning to follow the car. If you fail to make the observation, you should relax and repeat the experience. Some persons report that they lack clear visual images, noting the tenseness as if to follow the car but not seeing a car in imagination. If you have been successful, you are to imagine (with intervening periods for relaxation

of the eyeballs) various other simple objects, moving or
stationary, such as a train passing, a bird flying, a flower
fluttering in the wind, a tall tree or tower, a ball rolling
on the ground, a triangle, a square, a circle, a point, a blade
of grass and a sailboat in the distance. As you gain skill
in noting slight ocular tensions, you may assign yourself
a more complex task, such as observing the experience
when you recall the morning newspaper or when you perform a simple problem in arithmetic or when you think
of some social or business matter. In each case, as a rule,
following adequate training at observing, most persons
report that their visual images are accompanied by sensations in the eye muscles as if from looking at the object
imagined.

As far as possible you should not assume that this book
is correct in stating that eyeball tensions accompany visual
images, but should test this matter for yourself. In medical
practice, the physician does not even hint to the patient
that he is to look for tensions during visual imagination—
for leading questions are omitted where it is desired to
conduct an investigation scientifically. Even if the desire
is only for therapeutic results, it is better to have the
patient rely on his own observations.

The instruction which you are to follow is to "cease to
move the eyes in any direction or to look forward, yet not
to hold them still: you are to relax the eyes in the same
manner as you relax the biceps".

Upon relaxing your eyeballs completely, avoiding such
slight tensions as take place even during imagination, you
will doubtless find that the mind ceases to be active. This,
then, is a desired form of mental control.

We now pass on to other muscular regions, recalling again that one such region is enough for practice at any particular hour period. If you are unsuccessful at observing tenseness in any region, it is best to relax as completely as possible for a few minutes before repeating the experience.

Upon closing your jaws tightly, you should note tenseness extending from the angle of the jaws up to the temples. Opening the jaws produces tenseness which you may locate approximately in front of the ears but deep within the tissues. You are to show your teeth, noting tenseness in the cheeks (not in the lips, where there is a different sensation). Rounding the lips as in saying "Oh" is accompanied by sensations of tenseness in the lips. Retracting the tongue should call to your notice tensions in the tongue itself as well as in the region behind the chin, called the "floor" of the mouth.

If you have carried out the foregoing instructions, you are now prepared for practice on speech. After the customary five to fifteen minutes of preliminary relaxation, you are to count aloud to ten, sufficiently slowly so that you may observe what takes place. After a sufficient number of repetitions, you should perceive tension in your tongue, lips, jaw regions and throat, as well as vaguely in the diaphragm and all over the chest, as you produce each sound. If successful at these observations, you relax again for a while, then count half as loudly as before, when you should find that the same tensions recur but less strongly. Next you are to count similarly but so that you can scarcely be heard, making your observations. After further relaxation you are to count as before but this time not quite perceptibly, then less markedly than this and finally again less. According to reports, this becomes the same as when you imagine that you count from one to ten. The instruction now is to relax the speech apparatus completely—including the muscles of the tongue, lips, jaws, throat, chest and diaphragm. When you carry this out, you find that you no longer imagine in verbal terms—no longer speak to yourself.

Thereupon you may imagine or recall yourself speaking in various ways, such as telling a waiter to bring your dinner or requesting a conductor to let you off the car. The good observer reports that he has slight tensions in the tongue, lips or throat as he speaks in imagination (sometimes also in the muscles of the jaw and floor of the mouth), and he does not fail to mention tensions in the chest and abdomen from breathing, which varies in its periods and pauses according to the character of the imagined speech. Imagining sounds also has been found to be accompanied by tensions, usually in the eye muscles, as if to look at the source of the sounds.

In high nerve tension the trained individual reports many gross and vague tensions in various parts of the body, sometimes fragmentary and elusive—abortive acts starting to do now one thing, now another—often without harmony or adequate coordination. So the highly nervous person describes his inner feelings, corresponding with our outward observations of his muscle tensions—his restlessness, shifting, grimaces, tics and other manifestations. We are led to the view that what you call the "feeling of nervousness" largely consists of the varied sensations from the disorderly muscular tensions, voluntary and involuntary, that mark your responses to environment.

It requires extreme progressive relaxation of the muscles of the eyes and speech apparatus to diminish mental activities. Considerable practice is necessary. You are simply to let these muscles go completely in the same manner as relaxing the muscles of the arm (Fig. 20).

Training in the measures described above enables you to observe what you are doing when you fail to sleep, as well as when you are mentally overactive or worried or are otherwise disturbed. Enabling you to make these observations starts you on the route toward doing away with undesirable overactivities. When you think or worry or are excited, you see things in imagination or say things to yourself. According to numerous observations, by finding what region is tense and relaxing it promptly you mechanically remove the disturbing activity.

PROGRAM FOR GENERAL RELAXATION

After you have acquired a thorough understanding of what is meant by cultivating relaxation, it is recommended that you adopt a program of relaxing the various parts of the body. The following is a brief summary of such a program.

You are to assume a fairly comfortable position on a bed or wide couch, as described above, and then proceed as follows:

Right arm—practice one hour or more each day for about six days.

Left arm—continue to practice on the right arm and now at the same time also on the left arm one hour or more each day for about six days.

Right leg—continue to practice on both arms and now at the same time also on the right leg for nine days.

Left leg—continue to practice on all parts mentioned above and now at the same time also on the left leg for nine days.

Trunk—additional practice for three days.

Neck—additional practice for two days.

Forehead—one day.

Brow—one day.

Eyelids—one day.

Eyes—daily for one week.

Visual imagery—daily for one week.

Cheeks—one day.

Jaws—two days.

Lips—one day.

Tongue—two days.

Speech—three days.

Imagined speech—daily for one week.

Caution. Devote no more than the first portion of any period to learning to recognize tenseness in muscles, through the methods covered in the illustrations. The remaining time should be given over exclusively to complete relaxation. Never contract a part in order to relax it. *Avoid movements as an aid* during attempted relaxation; but also avoid holding still by a slight continuous tension, since this is not relaxing but only a useless imitation.

14

How to Relax While Active

"Learn to relax" originally meant to Mr. Doe merely
that he should rest at frequent intervals. He did not
see why he should need a doctor to aid him to carry out
this prescription. When, during the early weeks of treatment, the doctor seriously undertook to teach him to let go
muscle by muscle, while lying down, he wavered between
uncertainty as to what it was all about and doubt that it
was worth-while. At times he was tempted to question the
doctor's judgment and even sincerity. It was all so different from what he had come to regard as standard medical
treatment for his condition—taking sedative medicines or
listening to counsel and reassuring talk! At times he felt
ill as well as discouraged; nevertheless the doctor continued impassively to teach him the next step, apparently
understanding his complaints but evading his attempts
to discuss them. There were other times when he felt better and ascribed his improvement to the treatment. Somewhat to his amazement the doctor greeted his enthu-
siasms no more cordially than his unfavorable opinions.
He was encouraged only to maintain an open mind, to

refrain from jumping at conclusions and to wait to pass judgment until he had learned to observe for himself. Above all, he was to practice regularly each day. On the whole, he was reminded of his experiences in school; he was receiving a course of instruction on how to behave when lying down. It differed from all the courses he had taken in school chiefly because the instructions were negative in effect. He was being taught merely *not* to do anything while attempting to rest. After all, it was very simple.

Although the doctor did not prophesy results, Mr. Doe, let us assume, believed that his sleep was becoming more restful at least on some nights, shortly before or after he had learned to relax his eyes fairly well; and at moments when he seemed to himself relaxed, he noticed for the time being a certain abatement of some of his former symptoms.

It seemed quite interesting when for the first time he was informed that today he was to sit up but that he should relax so far as possible in this posture. Because the muscles of his back and of certain other regions had to be tense in order to maintain the sitting position, while other muscles were relaxed, this was called "differential relaxation". He wished to ask various questions about differential relaxation, but instead, the doctor encouraged him to observe for himself. Here, however, we need not hold back and so shall try to answer some of the questions Mr. Doe had in mind.

Perhaps his thoughts ran something like this: Before I took this course of treatment, I used to think of golf, billiards, the movies or some other form of recreation when I heard or read the word "relaxation". Now I have learned that for me at least the greatest relief from nervous strain comes when I lie down and let my muscles go completely in the manner I have been taught. It seems reasonable to assume that if I do this for an hour or two regularly each day, I should get somewhere in the course of time toward a calmer and quieter disposition. I am probably right in believing that I am sleeping better than before I began to take lessons. But I do not understand how anything more can be done or what is the purpose of my sitting up and being trained to relax in that position.

The doctor is accustomed to questions of this kind. Sometimes they come from persons (even a few doctors) who do not wish to consider evidence—being certain that learning to relax has nothing to do with overcoming nervous and other ills except insofar as the patient *believes* that benefit will result. With such persons, further discussion is perhaps better omitted. Consolation may be found in Aristotle's advice that one should limit one's arguments to those who are actually in doubt and who seek the truth, rather than include those whose chief need is sharpened wits. Since John Doe belongs to the former class, the doctor reminds him how often in the past he has acted excitedly at a time when he might have carried out the same task in a calm manner. Such calmness under the circumstances would be called "differential relaxation". Or perhaps after some loss on the stock market or other misfortune, Mr. Doe tried to conceal his regrets but felt a strong inward emotion (which could have been detected by electrical tests). If he had greeted the loss with a reasonable degree of placidity, *inward* as well as *outward*, it would be an instance of differential relaxation.

To this John Doe replies, "I understand a little better what you mean, but can you give me more convincing illustrations?" Learning to dance, states the doctor, offers many illustrations. At first you moved stiffly and made unnecessary movements, then as you progressed you went through the same steps but let your limbs and trunk relax to a much greater extent. That was an instance of progressive differential relaxation.

To what has been said we may add that tests have been carried out on university students during such customary activities as reading and writing to see what happens under conditions favorable to relaxation. It was found that while they continued at the task their knee-jerks soon began to diminish, showing that their legs were relaxing. (The knee-jerk is the kick seen when a rubber tipped hammer strikes the tendon below the kneecap, provided that the thigh has been supported and that the leg and foot dangle freely.) The same tests on subjects previously trained to relax indicated that during periods when they were requested to relax these individuals showed a much more marked relaxation of the lower limbs while reading and writing than they did during periods when they were not so requested. These investigations afford evidence that some degree of relaxation frequently takes place during reading, writing and other customary activities in normal persons under favorable conditions and can be specially cultivated, if desired.

In a group of young women electrical measurements were made in the muscles which extend the leg. The legs hung freely while they read copies of a certain magazine. After about two months, during which they were instructed to relax their limbs in seven periods of treatment, the tests were repeated. Although instruction had been given only in the lying posture, a marked decrease in muscular tension was found as they sat reading the same magazine. Evidently they had become accustomed to be more relaxed, in their legs at least, under the conditions of reading. Other subjects, used as controls, who had received no training but who were tested similarly, showed no decline in tension, permitting the conclusion that the training had been effective. Such investigations lead us to believe that training can effect an economy of muscular energy during reading and other activities.

In various arts a type of relaxation has long been sought, although previous to the present studies it went unnamed. Teachers of speech and of singing, including the operatic type, devote much time to the relaxation of the muscles of the throat, larynx and respiratory organs. Singers early learn that a loud tone is not required in order to be heard in the back row of an auditorium with good acoustics. "Carrying power" of voice, as it is called, increases not alone with loudness but particularly also when the voice is properly placed. Even a whisper should be so uttered as to carry to the last row. It is commonly understood that voice placement depends largely upon proper relaxation. Generally the student is taught to locate his breathing expansion in the lower portion of the thorax (chest). When the lips, tongue and jaw are in the proper position for utterance, a minimum requisite of breath is expressed, chiefly from the lower part of the thorax. The student is particularly taught to sing with the throat and jaw muscles relaxed as much as possible. He is not to sing or speak "from the mouth", or carrying power will be lacking. Likewise, the timbre of the voice somewhat depends upon proper relaxation. The so-called throaty tone, which may mar a performance, is due to excess tension in throat and laryngeal muscles. Unfortunately, vocal teachers commonly lack an adequate knowledge of anatomy and physiology, which doubtless would greatly expedite their work.

In aesthetic and ballet dancing relaxation plays a conspicuous role. The individual who holds himself rigid in these arts fails in his effects. A particular exercise is repeated until grace is attained. This means that those muscles alone are used which are needed for the act and that no excess tension appears in them or in others. Delsarte undertook to prove that relaxation underlay the art of sculpture, indeed all the physical arts, and developed his so-called decomposing exercises in order to secure his aim. Certain philosophical works on aesthetics seem somewhat to realize these points, but they fall short of clear, well-defined statements.

There is evidence, then, that a person may be more or less excited—more or less tense—in various muscle groups during action. When a person acts with absence of excessive tenseness, we call his state "differential relaxation". *This term accordingly means the minimum of tensions in the muscles requisite for an act, along with the relaxation of other muscles.* A large variety of instances of differential relaxation can be found in daily life. The speaker with a trained voice does not tire even after prolonged effort if he keeps his throat differentially relaxed. The billiard player spoils the delicate shot if he is generally too tense. The golf or tennis player learns to mingle a certain relaxation in strokes that are successful. The restless or emotional student finds it difficult to concentrate. The excited salesman fails to impress his prospective client. The clever acrobat produces an impression of grace and ease by relaxing such muscles as he does not require. The comedian often makes his ludicrous effects depend upon the extreme relaxation of certain parts of his body while others are active or held rigid. It seems safe to say that every learning process depends upon the acquisition of certain tensions with concomitant relaxations. Textbooks of psychology commonly illustrate the early learning process by the child at the piano, who squirms and shifts, perhaps even protrudes his tongue, when the notes are first studied. As skill is acquired, these tensions disappear: a certain degree of differential relaxation sets in.

With care you can observe excess tension in people around you every day. There are individuals who gesticulate unnecessarily, speak rapidly or with a shrill pitch, shift or turn about excessively, wrinkle their foreheads or frown too often, move their eyes unduly or show other signs of overactivity or excitement. Interesting imitations of high nervous tension in normal individuals under conditions of excitement can be found in almost every current exhibition of the motion pictures. Obviously, however, stagecraft is successful in its imitation of human activity in proportion as the total muscular patterns, including both tensions and relaxations, are duplicated.

In medical practice it has usually seemed simplest and most convenient to show the patient how to relax while lying down before training him in differential relaxation. For the treatment of chronic cases both types of training appear to be necessary, because the individual who remains excited during his daily activities does not readily relax when lying down. The tensions appear to be cumulative in their effects. For instance, according to modern experience the individual who has had insomnia for many years needs to be shown how to avoid not alone restlessness at night but also undue excitement during the day. Conversely, the nervous, excitable individual needs to be shown not only how to be relaxed while at his activities but also how to avoid restlessness at night if sleep is to be made profound and restorative.

You are, therefore, to continue your daily practice lying down while you learn to form the new habit of being relaxed in the upright posture. A convenient way to begin is to relax thoroughly for fifteen to thirty minutes on a couch and then to shift slowly, with limply hanging limbs and head, to a near-by chair. You then relax all parts of your body in this new posture as well as you know how, keeping the eyes closed. You are to maintain sufficient stiffness of the back to prevent falling off the chair, but no more.

In the sitting posture a review of the same procedure as that followed while lying down is now initiated. Some nervous individuals at first desire the support of a pillow, but this is to be omitted as soon as possible. Keeping your eyes closed, bend your left arm; you should now be able to recognize distinctly the sensation of tenseness in the front part of the upper arm, even if no one helps you by holding the arm back and even if now you bend it only slightly (see Fig. 21). Having succeeded at this, let the left arm fall at your side, to rest fairly comfortably on some portion of the chair. The remainder of the first hour period of differential relaxation may be devoted to letting the left arm become as limp as possible and maintaining it so.

On the following day you take the next step in a similar manner, extending your left forearm as in Fig. 4, but preferably without the use of books. If your forearm has been resting on the arm of your chair, bent at the elbow, move the wrist (with hand limp) so that the arm slowly becomes straightened. This permits you to observe the sensation in the rear of the upper arm when the triceps muscle contracts. Your practice most likely will be thorough if you devote the first portion of each hour period to recognizing the muscle sensation during a particular contraction and the remaining portion of the period to discontinuing this particular contraction. Day by day you are to repeat in a sitting position contractions of muscle groups in the same order as was followed in the previous chapter.

At this stage an experienced observer can readily tell if you are not well relaxed. If you are not, he notes that you sit with your head only partly bent over, the eyelids wink at times as in thinking or the limbs appear somewhat stiff. From time to time you may shift your position because of mild discomfort, but no such need arises, as a rule, during successful relaxation. If motionless but not well relaxed, you will probably discontinue your practice before an hour has elapsed, complaining of fatigue. The onset of fatigue during the attempt to relax clearly suggests that the directions given here are not being followed correctly.

In preparing to relax the back, sit erect and note the

sensation of tenseness along both sides of the spine. Having done so, you are to cease to be tense in these regions, letting go as far as you can without actually falling over or leaning uncomfortably far forward or backward. Upon coming to the muscles of the neck, you should note not alone the tension in moving or inclining the head in any direction but also the slight static tension present when the head is held upright in ordinary posture. When the head droops during a prolonged period of relaxation in a sitting position, the subject generally complains at first of pain in some portion of the neck from ligaments that are being extended. This need not concern you, since adaptation usually sets in after a week or more of practice, and the pain diminishes or disappears.

Prior to experience with the method of relaxation, patients of a nervous type very often complain of a dull ache in the back of the neck or just above this region, in the head. Not infrequently the patient, after learning to recognize the experience of muscular contraction in the aching region, volunteers that the pain evidently arises from continued contraction there. Another type of ache or pressing distress due to chronic muscular contraction is called the "tension headache", which sometimes seems to be located at the top of the head. As the patient learns to relax the muscles of the forehead and brow, the pains may disappear—without suggestion from the physician that they will disappear and without his indicating what possibly has been their cause. You may have had similar experiences in the regions just mentioned or in others. But even if you learn to relax such regions and the distress disappears, you should be cautious in drawing conclusions as to what was the source of pain. Under similar circumstances the careful physician also is guarded in his reasoning.

It is particularly important to repeat the tensions of the eyes and the speech organs and to relax these anew in the sitting posture. According to the reports of many subjects, there occurs for a time a diminution of mental and emotional activity. Your purpose is to try to set up modified habits—"conditioning" yourself, as some call it—in the direction of greater nervous quiet when sitting up.

Steady tensions may require special practice to relax. Even an experienced individual may continue to be somewhat rigid in a part which he believes to be quite relaxed. To learn to recognize the presence of tensions in such localities and to let them go step by step marks an important stage in learning to relax.

When the subject has become expert, his posture is typical (Fig. 22). The legs are more or less sprawled out and move limply if an observer pushes them. The arms and head droop flaccidly, and the trunk may be bent in any direction. Breathing is regular and quiet. There is no trace of restless movement, even of a finger. A certain flattened or toneless appearance is characteristic of the eyelids, which do not wink during a prolonged period. This must be sharply distinguished from an earlier stage when the eyelids are held motionless for a time, followed by vigorous winking of the closed lids. Close observation should reveal no motion of the eyeball. To carry out these procedures properly, you will need the assistance of some person, who must learn to observe you carefully and to criticize you accordingly.

If you have been successful up to this stage, you are now to learn to relax the eyes partially. You have previously learned to let the eyes go completely, so that they are not looking in any direction. But you cannot continue this with open eyelids for any considerable period because of a burning sensation due to the absence of winking and of adequate moistening of the eyeballs. Therefore, as a new practice, you are to permit the eyes to wander about to a slight degree, not letting them relax extremely. When this is done, a moderate amount of winking occurs, preventing discomfort and securing relative rest. Daily practice at complete relaxation of the eyeballs with closed lids and at partial relaxation with open lids may sooner or later lead you to feel that your eyes seem more rested; but such subjective impressions are not trustworthy unless sustained by findings of a careful oculist. We do not here seek to help you to "throw away your glasses", as is promised in certain books, which not alone make unwarranted claims but also do not even advance correct methods to produce extreme ocular relaxation.

The above described methods of resting your eyes can be frequently applied at odd moments during the day. From time to time during prolonged reading it is probably good practice to rest them briefly in this way.

Various periods of practice are devoted to reading. You are now to read, while relaxing the lower limbs; the back, so far as sitting posture permits; the chest, so far as can be done while inner speech continues; and the arms, so far as is possible while they hold the book or magazine. With the forehead and eyes extremely relaxed, you will of course not read. But you should relax these parts while holding the reading matter in order to become familiar with an extreme form of differential relaxation. A little more tension is then introduced; the words are to be read, but the eyes and other parts are to be kept as far relaxed as possible at the same time. Perhaps you find that you now follow the words but fail to get the meaning. This still represents too great a degree of relaxation. Accordingly, you are to read again, this time engaging in just enough contractions to get the meaning clearly but not more (Fig. 23).

These practices require the development of considerable skill, and the presence of an experienced critic is doubtless essential for the attainment of best results. But if the reader can succeed in securing even a slight measure of improvement in efficiency, he may perhaps consider his time well spent.

The effect of such practice, under medical direction (as tested by electrical measurements and certain other methods), is to tend to bring about a quieter state of body during reading, writing and other sedentary occupations (Fig. 24). According to reports, fatigue diminishes. Apparently restlessness, even if unnoticed, may interfere with attention and memory. This is perhaps because a generally tense state of muscles arouses sensations from these muscles which inhibit orderly thinking. Sometimes after relaxation has been learned, the patient asserts that he is able to work under noisy or otherwise irritating conditions, which formerly discomfited him. He may report less fatigue than formerly after working, and perhaps also a generally increased efficiency. The accuracy of these reports has not yet been tested in the laboratory. My clinical impressions, which have little value as evidence but which serve to lead toward further investigations, are that in the course of weeks or months the individual's demeanor as well as countenance shows a change; his movements lose their quick, jerky habit; his voice becomes quieter and his speech slower; and lines of fear become less marked, as his anxious or worried appearance gives way to a more placid and restful expression.

When you read or write or are otherwise employed, certain activities evidently are an essential part of the process. These are called *primary* activities. Included among these are the contractions of those muscles needed for maintaining posture, for holding a book or pen, for moving the eyes to follow the print, and in most persons for moving the tongue and lips to repeat the words in inner speech. While all these primary activities join in the performance of a task, certain others may be observed in the average individual which apparently do not contribute but rather detract from his performance. These are called *secondary* activities, since they are not at all needed for the task in hand. Innumerable examples come to mind: while reading, a noise in the next room may be followed by the individual's looking up and turning the head in that direction. Almost any distracting sound or sight may be followed by such secondary activity. Very often while reading or otherwise engaged the average individual is subject to an undercurrent of distracting thought processes in the form of worries, reflections, irrelevant recollections, intentions to do this or that thing; even songs or strains of music are silently but almost incessantly repeated. Many if not most persons read in this way, so that perfect attention to a book or occupation, even for so brief a time as a few minutes, is found perhaps only among those select individuals who have attained or are attaining eminent skill in their field.

Relaxation during activity should be applied to both primary and secondary activities. Primary activities may be unnecessarily intense for their purpose. For instance, a person may sing too loudly, pound his fist too vigorously as he converses, peer too intently, overexert himself in study. In such instances a better result will be produced by not trying so hard, by relaxation of primary activities. This relaxation should be carried only to the point where maximum efficiency continues; beyond this it would interfere with the purpose in hand. However, the aim is to carry relaxation of secondary activities to the extreme point, since these activities are generally useless.

We can briefly restate the substance of this chapter. In principle, vigorous activity is not precluded but rather is favored by a certain economy in the expenditure of neural and muscular energy. There is growing evidence that the average person whose organs are sound but who is nervously irritable and excited can learn to control these states by relaxing while he continues to engage in his daily affairs. As a result, it is now possible for many persons suffering from so-called nervous breakdowns to be spared the necessity of giving up their business, averting the additional worry and loss which they sustain when ordered to take the old-fashioned "rest-cure" or to "leave town for a change".

PROGRAM FOR DIFFERENTIAL RELAXATION

After you have made yourself familiar with what is meant by relaxation during activities, it is recommended that you adopt a program of regular practice in relaxing the various parts of the body as far as possible while sitting up in a chair. Following is a brief summary of such a program.

Left arm—practice one hour or more each day for about six days.

Right arm and other parts—as related on pages 122 to 123, inclusive.

Sitting up, eyes open—relax eyes extremely till they burn; then close them. Repeat. One day of practice.

Sitting up, eyes open—relax eyes partially, permitting them to wander somewhat for two days of practice.

Reading—practice for two days or more.

Writing—practice for two days or more.

Conversing—practice for two days or more.

In addition to your practice one hour each day, try to keep in mind the aim to relax, as far as you can with undiminished efficiency, while engaged in your daily activities. See what you can do toward improving your game of golf through relaxation. By applying what you have learned, try to avert strain and fatigue in your arms and legs while driving your car. If you are a salesman, practice keeping your arms and legs relaxed while meeting customers. Perhaps you have discovered that there are certain muscles which you contract unnecessarily while at work and which you can relax instead.

15

Instruction by the Doctor

Although this volume is addressed chiefly to healthy
individuals and to persons who lack opportunity for
medical consultation on matters of tension and relaxation,
we pause now to ask how the doctor can aid, and when
and why he is needed.

During the course of treatment by relaxation, as by any
other method, symptoms of disease generally arise from
time to time which require diagnosis, particularly in regard to whether they are appropriately treated by methods of relaxation. Obviously such questions require the
attention of a competent physician, even if preliminary to
taking up relaxation the patient has had a thorough physical examination.

But this is not all. The claims of any manual on relaxation must be modestly stated. As a rule, physical arts are
not well learned from books alone but require personal instruction and example. To illustrate, a person may in some
instances learn to play the piano or violin by himself, but
his technique is likely to be inferior and therefore his ac-
complishments limited. This is particularly true in learning

to relax. A physician is needed to point out to the patient when and where his tensions occur, to direct him where particularly to relax and to inform him whether he is succeeding or failing. (In determining this, electrical measurement is now a very important aid.) After training, the patient becomes better able to observe these matters for himself. But first old habits need to be overcome, and the patient commonly needs outside assistance to do this. Furthermore, he undertakes a difficult task when he starts to teach himself and is likely to become tense in certain respects in so doing. Skill in recognizing the experience of tension and its locality can be developed, I believe, if the directions given in Chapter 13 are followed with care and patience. But not everyone will succeed in this independently, particularly under conditions of excitement or distress. In many instances of nervous disorder, judgment and self-control are impaired to such an extent that professional guidance is indispensable. While to most persons the sensation in a contracting muscle is a familiar experience, yet the fainter forms of this experience, so helpful in controlling relaxation, are most readily recognized with the aid of personal instruction.

Even the simple acts illustrated in the figures of Chapter 13 are seldom properly performed by most patients until after repeated instruction. For example, upon bending the right arm, they persist in holding the wrist stiff at the same time, thereby frustrating the attempt to effect contraction in one group of muscles as exclusively as possible. Again, when requested to cease contracting, many bring the hand back to the couch by contracting another set of muscles, instead of simply letting go those muscles that were contracting. Correction of such errors obviously is most readily effected with the aid of the observing eye of an experienced physician. Many other such technicalities could be mentioned which hinder the progress of the patient unaided by personal instruction. There is also always the possibility that the individual, distracted as he is by other matters, will overlook his own tensions at particular moments and in impatience will give up the whole procedure.

While doubtless it is better than no rest at all, there is abundant evidence from clinical experience that the daily nap alone, so often recommended for the control of nervous and mental disorders, insomnia, colitis, high blood pressure and other serious conditions, has marked limitations. In many instances patients who for years have taken daily rests nevertheless come to the physician with conditions of high nerve tension or one of the other disorders mentioned. Indeed, even the patient who has been bedridden for years may be habitually overemotional and unrelaxed. Accordingly, it seems far from safe to assume that lying down each day in the hope of obtaining rest is equivalent to methodical treatment by relaxation.

Studies published in 1942 illustrate the failure of daily rest alone, without any training to relax, to reduce high nerve tension in certain cases. Measurements were made on six persons who were suffering from high nerve tension although according to their reports they had rested each noon or afternoon during one or more hours for at least six months. Two were physicians; one was a doctor's wife. Their complaints were various but included (severally) fatigue, insomnia and high blood pressure as well as nervousness. Not alone did their symptoms show no clear signs of abatement, but electrical measurements showed in five cases out of six that their failure to relax was no less striking than that of another group of highly nervous persons who had not rested daily.

Another impediment to self-instruction by the patient is the fact that he possesses no objective standard by which to judge his own improvement or deterioration. The opinion of the patient himself in this respect cannot be trusted. He is likely to be overenthusiastic or depressed at any particular time, and his views are likely to change. Past symptoms are likely to be forgotten or exaggerated in their intensity, if he relies upon his own judgment and recollection. Scarcely more reliable are the opinions on his condition passed by members of his family and his friends. Testimonials are to be disregarded as more befitting advertisements of patent medicines or the claims of pseudoreligious cults than a scientific method carefully pursued. The doctor may show reasonable interest in the patient's reports on his own symptoms; but to be sure that improvement has really occurred, objective data are required, whether secured by electrical measurements, X-rays or other procedures suitable to the particular condition of the patient.

In his attempts to learn, the patient is aided by correction when he errs and by an "O.K." when he succeeds. Without such aid, I have found, he is often mistaken as to whether he has been successful and consequently may fall into wrong habits of tension or become unduly discouraged. This again is essentially what happens in learning anything; the teacher's comments are directive.

It is true that for success in overcoming high nerve tension the patient must progress through his own endeavors; but this does not mean, as some would believe, that science has nothing to offer him. Similarly, to learn mathematics or a foreign language, your own efforts are required and independence is ever to be encouraged; but this does not mean that teachers are useless. Rather, competent teaching takes advantage of knowledge and methods gained in the past so that the individual is enabled eventually to proceed by himself better than if he had been exclusively his own teacher.

This practical procedure is, of course, different from the methods of Coué and the pseudoreligious cults which teach the sufferer to say "All is well", whatever the conditions. During treatment by relaxation reality is faced as such. The purpose is not to palliate the unavoidable hardships of life but to recognize them clearly and to live through them successfully. No attempt is made here to paint in joyful words what is plainly a source of misery. Rather, the aim is to reduce excess emotion so that adjustment can be made with such calm that health and efficiency are not seriously affected.

Patients who greet the physician as a great healer commonly make difficult pupils when learning to relax. They expect to lean on the doctor rather than to listen to his instructions and to follow them carefully. They are likely to ask him repeatedly for encouragement and for reassurance that their condition is not serious but is getting better. What is the doctor to do, if he desires to avoid methods of encouragement and suggestion? The author's method has been to ask the patient to see if during such concern he is tense somewhere and, if so, to try to relax the tension. It can not be too much emphasized that the present method is limited to instructions to relax muscles and does not include attempts to effect results by suggestions and reassurances.

Romance and imaginative appeal to patients are lacking in the method described here. Testimonial meetings, in which glasses and crutches are dramatically thrown away, do not occur. Improvement, when achieved, is a gradual growth and often is not accomplished so speedily as some patients demand. Often it is no more than wishful thinking to assume that one can get well fast. For those who need it most, there is no royal road to acquiring relaxed habits of living.

A difficult class of patients are those who, under treatment by the physician but not understanding the underlying principles, watch their symptoms from day to day or week to week in an endeavor to decide whether it is worthwhile to continue. When they feel better, they decide to go on; when they feel distressed or particularly fatigued, they are inclined to stop. Frequently such patients decide at a more advanced stage of treatment that their improvement has been sufficiently accomplished to make it unnecessary for them to continue. It then becomes the doctor's function to explain why their opinion is not to be relied upon.

A more intelligent patient attitude is illustrated in a subjective report from a physician who had been receiving treatment for overactive nerves along with symptoms of colitis. At the end of a six-month period, when he had been trained to relax lying down but not as yet sitting up, he stated that he no longer noted any of his previous symptoms but realized that it was for his physician to decide, on the basis of objective observations, when treatment should be terminated. Obviously none but an experienced physician is qualified to decide at what stage of improvement treatment can be discontinued without danger of relapse.

A course of treatment generally includes two or more hours of instruction per week. In addition the patient is required to practice alone one or two hours each day. The instructions are simple, and no attempt is made to arouse confidence in the good effects to be expected from the treatment. Skepticism is no hindrance, provided that the patient practices faithfully, except in instances where skepticism evidently signifies preconceived ideas and indicates a lack of understanding of instructions. An important function of the physician is "police duty"—seeing to it that the patient practices regularly. Again, there are certain individuals who relax well upon request (as shown by electrical measurements) but who become excited under stress. These individuals require frequent reminders until differential relaxation becomes habitual.

Considerable variation exists in the length of time required for the treatment of different individuals, depending upon their age, previous habits, ability to follow directions, regularity of practice and of course upon the character and duration of their particular disorder. According to my experience, the individual of average intelligence, if regular at his appointments, can learn to relax, at least to a marked extent, fairly quickly. Children old enough to follow simple directions make apt pupils. For them, instructions in how to recognize the experience of contraction in various muscles may be to a large extent omitted. Illustrations by the teacher, inducements through rewards and other devices may be necessary in handling younger children.

The method of relaxation has proved suitable for treatment also of people of advanced age, provided that the patient's cooperation is obtained. Previous training in dancing, singing, piano playing, athletics, physical education and other activities in which muscular arts are cultivated shortens the time required to learn to relax completely. Needless to say, disorders that have persisted for years require longer periods of treatment than those that have endured for a relatively brief time.

In the previous chapters were described methods for doctors and their patients and for those laymen who are perhaps on the road to developing physical ills but who have not yet arrived. In the present chapter we have shown why in the management of certain disorders a doctor is indispensable for adequate results not alone in diagnosis but also in cultivating relaxation.

16

Measuring Tension

In what has gone before, reliance has not been placed merely on observations on patients in the clinic. Quantitative measurements have been possible in certain important respects. Before going into these, it may be of interest to recall some of the historical background.

The past century has witnessed the rise and fall of many theories concerning neurotic disorder, its nature and its causes. Some of these views have been advanced by laymen or cultists, others by psychologists and physicians. One theory, which gained a firm foothold some fifty years ago, was based upon the observation that during fatigue people generally are more irritable than at other times; therefore, the nervous system must have become weakened by overuse. But laboratory workers have failed to find evidence that such weakness actually occurs. On the contrary, highly nervous persons often keep up a pace which their more phlegmatic neighbors fail to match.

Another theory, which became entrenched in the nineties and which at present is gaining new adherents, rests on the belief that we do not know why we act as we do when nervous; the cause of neurotic conditions, they say, is like the iceberg, of which but a small part is visible above the surface of the sea, much the greater bulk lying submerged. To discover the cause some analyst must delve into the secrets of our dreams and explore the hidden meanings of our acts. Adherents of this doctrine invariably trace the source of nervousness to matters of sex—particularly the sort of sex life and development which they believe that we had before and during early infancy.

The average physician in this country is kept too busy with visible matters of fact to have time to spare for fine-spun or fantastic theories concerning nervousness. Since an examination of the nerves and brain of nervous people, living or dead, as a rule discloses no tumor, no inflammation, no injury and no other alteration of structure which the skilled eye can detect, he has had until recently no tangible facts with which to work. But, lacking such facts and finding little appeal in speculative philosophies of any kind, many doctors have suspected that nervousness generally is secondary to other diseases or else is a sort of imaginary nothing. As one doctor recently commented, "It is only a state of mind".

Opposing the view that nervousness is merely an effect of other diseases are various well-known facts: that many children who are otherwise healthy are highly nervous; that adults differ widely as to how they meet the same disease conditions—some excitedly, others quite calmly; that the discovery and removal of a diseased tissue (such as a region of inflammation or tumor) in an excitable person commonly do not alter his nervous habits permanently; that in everyday life many events obviously give rise to highly excitable states of mind without any disease being involved. Such events are automobile and other accidents, including fires, where no personal injury occurs, illness or death of dear ones, loss of position or station or loss of fortune.

Amid the welter of conflicting theories concerning nervousness, attempts to get at the facts by established scientific procedures have been conspicuous by their absence. In this, as in other subjects, we should expect the genuine beginning of scientific progress to be marked not by the spinning of theories, but by the precise and orderly description of phenomena, followed as soon as possible by accurate measurement. Hoping to get somewhere by these methods, some fifty years ago I began a study of the start or jerk which some persons, nervous or otherwise, sometimes evince following a sudden noise or other strong excitation, usually while they are otherwise engaged. As is well known, extremely nervous persons often start on such occasions and sometimes report that they have had sensations of "shock". By means of a relatively crude device attached below the back of the neck, it was possible at that time very roughly to measure movements of the trunk. Tests in this manner readily confirmed the popular conception that persons showing other symptoms of nervous excitement often jerk violently when a sudden noise is made, particularly if they have been deeply engrossed on other matters.

Likewise, if the subjects, while sitting, were requested to hold the muscles of the limbs, head and trunk stiff, they generally started violently. This occurred not only with those who seemed highly nervous but with others as well.

When, on the other hand, the subjects relaxed their muscles as completely as they knew how, the start was generally diminished, the subject reported that there was
little or no shock and the sound seemed to lose its irritating
character.

So many muscles jerk during the nervous start that it
has not yet proved possible to record the agitation suitably
by mechanical means. Therefore in 1924 Miss Margaret
Miller, a graduate student, and I turned to a simpler act
for study. The subject lay upon a couch with eyes closed,
his right arm outstretched so that the finger tips made
contact with a little salt solution, through which we could
pass, when we wished, a momentary but painful electric
current. We were able to control the current in duration
and other essential characteristics so as to keep it constant
for each subject throughout all the tests. Each time the
subject felt the painful shock he withdrew his hand in
haste. Since his upper arm was fastened down, he could
withdraw the hand only by bending his forearm. We recorded the speed and extent of this movement.

In one set of tests the subject lay quietly, with eyes
closed, resting as persons ordinarily rest. In another set
of tests, alternating with the first set, he was requested to
relax extremely according to the methods I have described,
in which he had been trained for several months previously. For almost all of the subjects the results were
strikingly different in the two sets of tests: following the
instruction to relax extremely, the speed and extent of the
jerk as a rule were greatly diminished. One subject, who
relaxed most extremely as judged by other signs, did not
withdraw her hand at all as a rule in an entire series of

tests. Afterward she was amazed to learn that the strength of the shocking current was the same when she was extremely relaxed as when she was resting less quietly.

Such findings lead to interesting considerations. Individuals who start at sudden "shocks" naïvely try to explain their agitation as due to something outside of themselves, namely, the strong character of the disturbance. However, according to our tests, a violent reaction along with subjective distress seems to depend not only upon the exterior disturbance but also upon the preceding state of the muscles of the subject. Some individuals do not as a rule start visibly, but all withdraw their hands if the shock is sufficiently strong, provided that their muscles have been held moderately tense. On the other hand, as stated above, when the individual was extremely relaxed, the feeling of "nervous shock" was weak or absent, and the start, or withdrawal, was either absent or slight. These observations suggested the possibility that *all* subjective irritation or distress might be reduced if the individual were to become sufficiently relaxed; this hypothesis remains today a beacon light for further experiments and observations. A psychologist working in another laboratory has confirmed our finding that advanced relaxation tends to diminish certain types of pain.

The start is particularly marked in so-called irritable or excitable or nervous persons. It tends to be marked not alone in neuroses but also, as is well known, after operations and various forms of prolonged illness. Nervous individuals are not only easily disturbed by noises which tend to interrupt their train of thought, but they are distracted by many other types of stimuli (not necessarily sudden or unexpected) which do not affect phlegmatic individuals to the same degree. Events of little importance and pains from slight tissue changes are particularly likely to arouse distress in such individuals to the point of interrupting their useful pursuits. In fact, their subjective symptoms of distress appear to mount as they become increasingly irritated and excited. It seems probable that the physiology underlying this is a heightened nerve-muscle tension, which would readily account for many characteristics of individuals in a "nervous" state.

Perhaps the most commonly used test for nervousness is the knee-jerk, elicited by striking the tendon below the kneecap, while the thigh rests on a support so that the foot swings freely. The attention of the subject must be turned to other matters when the tap comes, or he is likely to hold the leg stiff, preventing the kick. Under these conditions if he is generally excited or if his muscles generally are in a state of moderate contraction, the kick is marked. But during extreme relaxation either in subjects previously trained to relax or in those who relax extremely without training, the kick is diminished or absent, as shown by Anton J. Carlson and the author in various tests.

By use of the methods described above, a certain movement may be repeatedly aroused in the subjects. In each case a disturbance in the sense organs is propagated through nerves to the central nervous system and then instantly back through other nerves to muscles, which thereupon are caused to contract. Such action is called "reflex". Arousing reflexes affords valuable information in the study of nervousness but is limited as a method of scientific investigation and leaves us without any standard of adequate measurement.

The problem faced in the author's studies some years ago was that persons might lie or sit outwardly quiet or almost so and yet show various clinical evidences of being nervously disturbed. Was it possible, for example, that an arm which appeared motionless to the naked eye nevertheless contained muscles engaged in slight but active contraction?

The beginnings of an instrumental approach to this problem had been laid by a very early investigator in animal electricity. In 1842 Carlo Matteucci, working on frogs' muscles, discovered that if he pinched a muscle or otherwise caused it to contract, he could detect at the moment of the contraction a faint wave of electrical current. Since that time workers in noted physiological laboratories all over the world have confirmed his discovery, making it seem probable that marked contraction of muscle can always be detected with electrical apparatus suitably sensitive. In 1907 another investigator in a German laboratory, H. Piper, first studied muscle contractions in man. His method was to have his subjects bend their right arm relatively quickly. My hope that the then newly developed vacuum tube would aid in these studies was particularly encouraged when, in 1921, Alexander Forbes and Catherine Thatcher, two investigators at Harvard University, first employed such tubes in the study of human muscle activities. During subsequent years, amplifiers have come to be widely used in the study of nerves and muscles. But the various equipment developed in 1927 evidently was not sufficiently sensitive to test whether or not a muscle, apparently in repose, was really giving off slight electrical currents, which would indicate a state of active contraction. I found it necessary to construct an assembly capable of measuring accurately such faint quantities as one millionth of a volt. In this task the Bell Telephone Laboratories very generously cooperated.

In making observations of the electrical impulses present in muscles during contraction, it was formerly necessary for accuracy to insert pins (of platinum iridium) into the muscles of the patient. Now these are omitted. Instead, I employ certain surface electrodes of the same metal. The minute electrical impulses must be amplified before they are strong enough to register on an indicator. In the recording instrument a wire less than one ten-thousandth of an inch in diameter extends for several inches in the field of a very powerful magnet. The wire is brilliantly illuminated, and its shadow, magnified six hundred times, falls on a screen, where it is photographed on a moving coil of paper. A permanent photographic record is thus secured of electrical changes in the particular muscle attached to the wires as those changes occur from instant to instant (see Fig. 25).

Most commonly the patient whose muscles or nerves are to be tested lies upon a couch in a darkened, quiet, partially soundproof room. He is requested to close his eyes and to relax as far as he knows how. Insertion of the very fine platinum wires disturbs him scarcely more than a pin prick, and as a rule he scarcely notices them after a very short time.

Under these conditions the patient whose nerves are

characteristically overactive, even if lying apparently motionless at the time the record is taken, shows clear evidences that his muscles are contracting. The fine wire in the indicator vibrates continuously or at irregular intervals at a high rate and often to a marked extent. If the instrument is set for high sensitivity, the vibrations may be so fast and large that they cannot be photographically recorded, and it becomes necessary to reduce the sensitivity, which can readily be done by turning a certain regulator. A photographic record from such a tense individual is seen in Fig. 27. For a short time the patient's arm muscles were completely relaxed, which produced the result shown in Fig. 26.

With the aid of this equipment it has been possible to test anew the thesis of this volume, that patients can be successfully trained to relax. From time to time, before, during and after the course of training, records were taken for half-hour periods and the results compared in a group of six highly neurotic patients. The results showed clearly that the subjects learned to relax. After the training to relax, most or all of the records are equivalent to a straight line on the photograph, like that in Fig. 26. The slight vibrations which still appear are due to a certain instability in the very delicate instrument itself and are present on records taken even if the wires connected with the subjects are short-circuited.

Tests show that a trained subject often can pass from marked tension to relaxation in as short an interval as one-fifth of a second.

What sort of records are secured from normal persons

not trained to relax? Tests performed on groups of college students showed that no student achieved and maintained complete relaxation of the arm muscles during the entire thirty minutes of rest. In a group of six the students showed approximately complete relaxation ranging from twenty to ninety-three per cent of the time. It is striking that a presumably normal individual, requested to relax completely, failed to do so for four-fifths of the time, notwithstanding that conditions were quiet and comfortable. This student described himself as at times "high-strung" and "excited". The one whose record showed him to be the most nearly relaxed stated that he had tried to train himself to relax. The records of the students as a group, while showing lower voltage than those of highly nervous patients before training, nevertheless failed to show the approximately complete relaxation seen in the neurotic patients after they had been trained to relax.

Similar measurements can be taken directly from the nerves of the patient by inserting the fine wire directly into the nerve. This also is a harmless procedure and requires no anesthetic. It is now possible, therefore, with the accuracy of the physical laboratory, directly to secure records of nerve and muscle states in patients. The result of the test on a patient can be expressed in a single number—expressing the mean voltage for the period.

Since the writing of the paragraphs which appear above, new instruments have been developed in the Laboratory for Clinical Physiology with the assistance of the Bell Telephone Laboratories. They have made it possible, for the first time in history, to measure electrical activity in

muscles or in nerves without photography. Each vertical
line (Fig. 27), representing contraction voltages in muscle,
is measured, summated and averaged over a period of time
such as ten seconds or two minutes, as the operator chooses.
So simple are the devices that he has but to look at an illuminated dial and record its movements as they occur at
regularly recurring intervals while the subject in an adjacent room attempts to relax or engages in any desired
activity. Measurements can be made simultaneously from
several regions of muscles or nerves as desired. The results,
after correction for constant errors, are readily presented
in graphs, which can be read plainly.

Nowadays I seldom insert wires directly into the muscles, the tension of which is to be measured. Improvements
in the circuit have made it possible to employ surface
electrodes instead. These are discs less than one-half inch
in diameter, made of platinum iridium with suitable at-
tachments so that they can readily be held against the skin
with small strips of scotch tape. Generally four sets of leads
are employed, making it possible to secure measurements,
for example, from selected regions of the arms, the legs,
the lower jaw and the eyes. Concurrent recordings from
these four regions are made over half-hour periods, while
the patient lies at rest or sits up with eyes either open or
closed. If such recordings are made from time to time, say
at monthly intervals, estimate can be made on the patient's
progress based upon objective findings.

Just as measurements of combustion in the body (basal
metabolism) have added to our knowledge in another
field of medicine, so it is believed that the methods above
described, if applied by physicians generally, offer a fruit-

ful source for future advances in the field of medicine. It would seem of extreme importance to the overcoming of nervous and mental disorders that every effort be made toward the development and promulgation of these accurate methods to replace the varieties of speculation now current in certain fields.

17

Relaxing the Mind

Even before World War I, a French physician, Dr. Laroussinié, called attention to the increase of nervous disorders in all countries. The psychopathic hospitals, public and private, were becoming insufficient to satisfy the demands made on them. He found the cause for these widespread nervous disorders in the "state of mind" that characterized the civil population: in the chasing after immediate wealth and material possessions which replaced the patient toil of our forefathers; in addiction to dances, alcohol and fast automobiles. These causes combined to raise new generations lacking in balance and self-control, impulsive and dangerous to society and to the state.

In a high-spirited people, like the American, ever on the alert toward new developments—financial, scientific, educational, artistic and social—we should naturally expect to find many minds overactive. Such advanced attainments generally come only after much thinking, and the rich and varied rewards offered in a lusty growing nation provide continual stimulation. The difficulties of the times and the efforts on all sides to reconstruct our economic system have, so to speak, only added fuel to our mental fires. Now we find ourselves facing an uncertain future which will require our clearest thinking and our fullest efforts if our liberties are to survive.

In a period marked by epochal changes, the life of each individual is necessarily affected. Adjustments to a more or less altered social order prove disturbing, adding to the problems which have to be met and tending toward the increase of high nerve tension. Under these conditions it seems safe to assume that almost any active individual has at times found himself obsessed by reflections and worries which he seemed unable to throw off. This applies to Americans but doubtless even more to unfortunates abroad. Various factors in modern life tending to incite excessive thinking and emotion have been sufficiently mentioned in earlier chapters. We are led to ask what can be done, if anything, to effect mental quiet amid all this turmoil.

Something like this question was on the tip of John Doe's tongue before he got very far in learning to relax. He began to recognize that possibly his bodily complaints such as his vague pains which he sometimes felt near the heart, the skipped beat, the discomfort in his abdomen due to what he called "gas", might be due to his muscular tensions, and he did not doubt that he would feel better in many ways if he really learned to relax. However, he realized that he worried too much and he considered this a trouble of his mind, not his body. At times he wondered whether he ought to go to work at all and occasionally he felt like dodging rather than meeting people. Often he did not seem able to concentrate as of old and his memory seemed impaired. More frequently than seemed good for him, he felt emotionally upset and sometimes even began to fear that he might pass into a state of panic.

He had read in many books that mental troubles commonly arise from failure to express your emotions. Maybe, he reflected, a fuller emotional expression was what he needed. He did not see that this would be provided however well he might learn to relax.

It is no wonder that John Doe had these misgivings. All of his life he had been accustomed to distinguish between his mind and his body. When he worried, he believed that he did so with his mind, not with his body. No doubt, he assumed, worry occurred as an act of the brain. To this extent, worry was something, he reflected, that went on in the body but it was within a particular part of the body, namely: the skull. What was true of worry, he believed, was likewise true of his memory and his attention, his fears and other emotions and especially his imagination. He yielded to the belief that mental activities occur in the mind and when muscles become tense, this is only a result or expression of what goes on in the mind. He maintained, therefore, that while relaxing might do him a lot of good, it could hardly be expected to take care of his mental ills. To this he added a further objection and difficulty. He found that when he was emotionally upset, he could not relax. From this he concluded that he lacked the will power to relax. From this objection he passed on to another, namely: that he could not be expected to relax in the presence of so much distress unless something was first done to improve his mental state.

John Doe came by his views honestly. He inherited them

from his forefathers, including those of the nineteenth century. As he learned to observe accurately what took place at moments when he worried, imagined, recalled or engaged in some other particular mental activity, he became enlightened. He acquired a new conception of what actually goes on during moments of worry and other mental activity. Experience taught him that the mind was not what he had believed it to be, following tradition. He acquired a new working conception and with the aid of a little explanation, he no longer assumed that whenever he worried it was an act of his brain alone. For one thing, he learned that as he relaxed, he ceased to worry! This surprised him!

Twenty-five years ago evidence that individuals could be trained to relax to the point of diminution or disappearance of worrying and other emotional overactivity would doubtless have received scant consideration. Most neurologists as a rule were not interested in the scientific study of mental processes. We then lived in an era of nervous medicine (not yet wholly past) which was skeptical rather than creative and therefore resistive rather than constructive. Its skepticism, moreover, was generally founded not on careful studies showing negative results, but on pseudo-authoritative dogmatism. Some physicians of the old school would have said that all instructions such as given here are mere "suggestions" to the patient and that the results are wholly due to his believing them. According to these physicians, wiggling a patient's right toe or giving him a bread pill would produce the same favorable result as relaxation and by the same means if the patient believed it would. They would have felt certain, without investigation, that lying down daily for an hour to relax without instruction would accomplish the same results as relaxing with instruction, provided that the patient believed it would.

Their view has not withstood the test of time, for I have shown that in many cases technical relaxation can succeed where daily rest alone has failed. In my tests two of the subjects were doctors; one was a doctor's wife. They stated that they had rested each afternoon over periods varying from six months to several years; however, they agreed that they had not become relaxed, and to this they attributed their complaints of fatigue, nervousness and insomnia. Electrical measurements confirmed their views, revealing that their muscles were continually contracting over prolonged periods of time, even while they attempted to relax.

The method of laboratory investigation teaches us to refrain from jumping at conclusions and makes it readily possible to arrange conditions from which the effects of "mental suggestion" can be excluded. Does muscular relaxation bear any relation to thinking, emotion and other so-called mental activities?

Investigations bearing on this problem were begun at the University of Chicago in 1922 and were continued there until 1936. Since then they have been conducted at my Laboratory for Clinical Physiology. Clinical records had been made previously in great detail. For scientific study it was of course necessary to consider only very simple types of mental activity, such as could readily be aroused in the laboratory when desired. The subjects had been trained to relax, as well as to report on their subjective experiences from muscular contractions.

Since the time of Francis Galton (1888) it has been known that all persons necessarily employ some images in their various forms of thinking, emotion and other mental activity. If you imagine a building or any other concrete object, you will probably see some sort of picture of it; this picture is relatively clear in some persons but in others is likely to be fragmentary, vague and fleeting. Some persons experienced in the scientific examination of their sensations report that they have few or no such visual images. Again, if they imagine or recall some sound, whether noisy or musical, most persons state that they seem to hear something more or less clear and perhaps have a vague sensation in the ear. When you imagine or recall tasting or smelling, reproductions in kind are likely to occur. Trained observers have generally agreed also that when they imagine or recall some muscular act they have an experience which seems faintly to reproduce or to resemble what takes place during the actual performance. Other sensations and feelings are often reproduced in us in much the same way. While, according to reports by experts, individuals differ greatly in the ability and extent to which they employ these various types of imagery, it is agreed, as said above, that everyone makes use of some types of images whenever he thinks. This point would be admitted even by certain students who hold that at certain significant moments our thinking is without images.

Accordingly, the subjects in our investigations, lying on couches under conditions favorable to relaxation, were at proper moments requested to imagine or to recall various simple matters and to describe what takes place at such moments. No subject was informed as to what the other reported; yet, following repeated observations, they practically all agreed that when they saw pictures in imagination or recollection, they simultaneously had faint sensations as if their eye muscles were contracting to look in the direction of the pictured object. Upon relaxing the eye muscles completely, they reported that the visual images subsided or disappeared. When requested to imagine counting to ten or to recall the words of a poem or something they had recently said, most of them stated that they had sensations in their tongue and lips and throat as if they were actually speaking aloud, except that they were much fainter and briefer. Upon relaxing the tongue, lips and throat muscles completely, most of them stated that imagining or recalling the numbers or words was discontinued. Some of the subjects believed that with relaxation of the organs of speech they still *visualized* numbers or words, but they agreed that sensations from the eye muscles seemed present at such moments. Following the instruction to relax completely the muscles of the eyes and of speech, all the subjects agreed that mental activity subsides or disappears. The investigator was careful to avoid suggesting his views to any subject. It was apparent in each instance that the observations were firsthand.

While the account given above is admittedly sketchy and incomplete, it will serve here to give a general idea of the manner and direction of our early investigations. Readers interested in a more precise account will find this in *Progressive Relaxation.*

What subjects report about their experiences, however technically they are trained to observe, is open to possible test if we have suitably sensitive instruments that can be appropriately applied. The possibility of detecting and measuring what takes place in the body at a moment of mental activity was the incentive that led to the development of the electrical apparatus previously described.

Here is an illustration. The subject lies relaxed upon the couch with eyes closed. He is instructed to engage in a particular mental activity at the first click of a telegraph key and to relax any muscular tensions present at a second signal. The wires attached to the electrical recording apparatus are inserted in the muscles that bend the right arm.

As previously stated, when a trained subject is instructed to remain relaxed, the fine wire (the movements of which are photographically recorded) remains quiet, producing an approximately straight horizontal line on the film. But when, for instance, the instruction is to imagine lifting a weight with the right forearm, the first signal is promptly followed by a series of long vibrations of the wire, which cease soon after the signal to relax. However, when the instruction is, "Imagine lifting with the left arm" or "Imagine bending the left foot", no electrical changes are recorded from the right arm, and the wire remains quiet as during complete relaxation. It remains quiet during various other kinds of such critical tests, which are called control tests.

If the subject has been requested to imagine striking a nail twice with a hammer in his right hand, two series of vibrations generally occur with a short intervening interval of quiet in the wire. Beautiful registration is secured following instruction to imagine or recall some rhythmical act, such as shaking the furnace.

To register what takes place during visual imagery, the wires leading to the recording apparatus are inserted in a certain manner under the skin near the eye muscles. When the eyes turn in a particular direction, for instance up, a distinctive pattern is recorded on the photograph. Upon instructing the subject to imagine particular visual objects, characteristic patterns are also recorded in most instances. For example, the pattern upon imagining the Eiffel Tower is the same as that for looking up. The conclusion seems justified that when you see visual pictures in imagination or recollection your eye muscles actually contract—however slightly—just as they do to a larger degree when you actually see; that is, you actually look in the direction of the imagined object. Furthermore, just as you exercise control on what you see by directing your gaze this way or that, you likewise control your imagination and course of thinking, at least with respect to the visual elements.

In certain studies fine wires have been inserted into the tongue, lips or region of the vocal cords to test muscles of speech during various types of thinking. If the subject imagines counting or recalls the words of a poem or song, a specialized pattern is in each instance photographically recorded. Even when he thinks of certain abstract matters, such as the meaning of the term infinity, there is evidence in many instances that his vocal organs move in a slight and abbreviated manner as if they were actually saying words. While these investigations are by no means complete, they already furnish strong evidence that our mental activities, in addition to images and perhaps other elements, essentially involve what might be called faint and abbreviated muscular acts. There has been abundant

evidence in these as well as in many other of our clinical
studies that with the relaxation of such muscular acts, the
entire process of thinking practically ceases for brief
intervals.

When a patient worries or engages in other disturbing
mental activities, we may profitably ask him, if he has been
adequately trained to report, what takes place at such moments. He states as a rule that he has visual and other
images concerning the matter troubling him and slight
sensations, as from eye-muscle and other muscle tensions,
while he sees and otherwise represents to himself what the
trouble is about. We have grounds for assuming that such
reports in general probably are substantially true, since
electrical methods have confirmed the presence of muscular contractions during such mental activities as have been
tested up to date. Admittedly, however, certainty on these
matters must await the application of electrical tests specifically to worry and other disturbed states. During extreme worry, fear or general emotional upset, the investigator who attaches his wires to any nerve or muscle will
generally find the part in a varying state of high tension
(technically speaking, marked action potentials can be
detected).

If the reports mentioned are scientifically upheld, two
ways seem open in clinical practice toward ridding the
patient of worry and other disturbing mental activity. One
is to train him to relax generally; the other is to train him
to relax specifically the tensions involved in the particular
mental act of worry or other disturbance. In general relaxation a stage is reached when, as can be noticed, the eyeballs cease looking, the closed lids appear flabby and free

from winking, the entire region of the lips, cheeks and jaws seems limp and motionless, and breathing shows no irregularity. Interrupted after such an experience, the trained patient reports that for the time being he was free from mental disturbance, since all imagery had indeed ceased. Such reports have been secured from a number of patients who were not told in advance what to expect; to some the results came as a surprise, since they had previously failed to see how relaxing muscles alone could have any bearing upon their mental problems. If it is true that maintaining general relaxation succeeds in markedly reducing, perhaps to zero, disturbed mental states, it seems reasonable to expect that with repetition and practice relief can be made more nearly permanent. This attempt has been described by Professor Anton J. Carlson as the reverse of the method of habit formation studied by Pavlow and his associates in Russia. While their work consists in forming new habits, here the attempt is to undo old connections.

The second way to train the patient to free himself from a particular form of anxiety or other disturbance requires that he first learn to observe and report accurately his sensations. He is then to practice relaxing the muscular tensions characterizing a disturbed state at the same time that he goes about his daily affairs. This is, again, differential relaxation. For example, a person may find himself continually recalling events in which he lost financially, thus disturbing his present efforts to work. If such disturbing reflections are found to include visual pictures of those events along with sensations as from eye muscles tensed to look at the pictures, the instruction is to relax such tensions while not closing the eyes and not otherwise ceasing to be active.

We see again the answer to the question, What have muscle tensions to do with worry, fear and other states of mind? Tests indicate that when you imagine or recall or reflect about anything, you tense muscles somewhere, as if you were actually looking or speaking or doing something, but to a much slighter degree. If you relax *these particular tensions,* you cease to imagine or recall or reflect about the matter in question—for instance, a matter of worry. *Such relaxations may be accomplished no less successfully while you are active in your daily affairs than while you are lying down.*

18

Common Nervous Disorders

"Nervousness" varies from time to time and from person to person like the waves of the ocean. But forms can be distinguished, and to these are given special names.

"High nerve tension" or "overactive nerves" are terms that seem to cover the forms which we meet most commonly. If you inquire and observe among your neighbors, you may be amazed to see how common nervous characteristics are—how seldom you find families free from them.

One person fails to sleep well; another (or the same one) is frequently overfatigued; a third worries almost incessantly; a fourth avoids long drives for fear of accidents; a fifth is unable to sit through a motion picture or the opera; a sixth is too restless to read and study as he formerly did; a seventh (and there are many sevenths!) is irritated and quarrelsome at home; an eighth is oppressed by his business duties and so on.

In all of these persons, as previously said, you can with care observe outward signs of excess tension—now in this muscle group, now in that. This excess tension obviously increases when the nervous symptoms become acute and commonly disappears when they subside.

In some of the foregoing examples one symptom or group of symptoms stands out. Perhaps it is nervousness during speaking: the individual stammers or stutters. If you inquire in detail, you find that the difficulties of each sufferer are somewhat specialized; each becomes particularly nervous or tense in saying—or in imagining that he is saying—certain sounds or in speaking to certain persons or in meeting particular types of situations.

Perhaps the outstanding symptom is fear, either reasonable or unwarranted.

Herbert Spencer maintained that without fear man could never have advanced beyond primitive states. Anticipation of future difficulties—however disagreeable—prepares the way to meet them with success. Thus fear is the great saver from harm, the great educator.

At a moment of marked fear, if our electrical recording instrument is suitably attached, currents are found to run high and frequent in almost any nerve or muscle. This is what we have called nervousness. If Spencer was right, nervousness at times can be very useful.

However, as any reader has witnessed, fears may become prolonged and excessive. Then they constitute a burden on the nervous system and may lead toward disorders in other systems as well. There comes a stage in certain cases where it becomes difficult to say whether the fear is merely an exaggerated normal state or a somewhat pathological one. But if the individual fears that he will jump out of a window when in high buildings or that he may stab somebody if a knife lies about, we call the fear definitely pathological and label it a *phobia*.

How does the method of relaxation apply to conditions of fear—normal or abnormal? The answer can be illustrated by the case history of an attorney who had amassed a small fortune, having lived a modern life of rush which involved protracted hours of attention to business. While still in his thirties, he complained that in so doing he had "burnt himself out"—had permanently impaired his vitality. Fatigue was frequently present, but most noticeable were fears, particularly when he was speaking at court or working in high buildings.

It is not considered sufficient in treating such a condition through relaxation for the patient to learn to be relaxed merely when lying down. Rather, it seems necessary for the patient to learn to recognize when and where he is tense during the experience of fear and to relax the localities involved. This is differential relaxation. Accordingly, this patient, after he had learned to relax very well lying down, as confirmed by electrical records, was trained to relax while sitting. His powers of observation were cultivated until he became able to report—without leading questions—what experiences he had at moments of fear. He said, for example, that when near a window in a high building he had visual images of himself jumping out, along with tensions in the eye muscles as in looking toward the window, but also with tensions in the limbs as if withdrawing from the window. Assuming that his observations were substantially correct, the physician instructed him to relax all such tensions, including those of withdrawal, at the moment of fear. At first the patient complained that his relaxation was not quick enough. During treatment, without letting him know why, he was repeatedly instructed to imagine various objects falling and to report his experiences each time. On each such occasion he was instructed to relax the tensions reported as apparently belonging specifically to each experience of fear. In the course of months, according to his reports, he developed on the whole an increasing control of those tensions. He now states—ten years after concluding the treatment—that there has been no recurrence of fears.

It seems important to note that the patient's habits of working all day and long into the evening as a rule were not discontinued even during the period of treatment. He believes that he now is able to work more effectively by relaxing differentially. There is objective evidence that his fears subsided, for, following his course of treatment, he calmly moved his business to certain desirable office space located in the tower of a high building.

"Worry" is the complaint perhaps most often heard by the doctor in the field of nervous medicine. Can modern science contribute anything toward the solution of the problem of worry? In the past, most laymen and many doctors have been inclined to believe that the only way to remedy worry is to "remove the cause" and that the cause of worry lies solely in the difficulties which we meet in life. But what really *is* the cause? Is it solely in those difficulties, or is it also in ourselves? Doubtless the quickest way to effect a cure of a particular worry is to remedy the matter of concern; for example, to provide funds for those who worry about poverty. But too often such provision is not feasible. Furthermore, certain losses cannot be

remedied at all, for example, the death of a loved one. And
in every life, trying situations inevitably arise from time to
time. We are faced with the fact that practically the same
kind of dangers and losses will lead one person to extreme
worry and irritability but leave another relatively calm
and self-possessed.

Granted that worry is a subjective state which is incited
but not wholly caused by various matters which arise in
the lives of everyone, what can be done about it? In many,
worrying becomes a habit; reassurance and argument
commonly seem of little avail; the more the talk, the more,
at least in some cases, does the worry seem to recur. Most
persons tend to review the troublesome matter again and
again in an effort to find a solution, even if only the imaginative one, "It might have been different!" To escape
such thoughts, resort often is made to change of scene, to
distracting occupation, to exercise and baths, perchance
to drink or to sedative drugs; but most commonly the problems of the worrisome individual are not solved. If fortune
favors or if time heals the wound, a new source of distress
soon appears on the horizon—to be followed by another
and another. The worrying tendency persists and ever
finds something new to feed upon.

The physician of today must prepare himself to deal
with the problem of worry. *Many persons successfully
engaged in useful occupations find themselves in need of
treatment.* It is extremely doubtful that methods of reassuring or of distracting them are sufficiently effective.

In training nervous persons to relax, the patients are
directed, as previously indicated, in methods of observing
what they do subjectively when they worry. They note

tensions of which, as they assert, they have been previously unconscious. As illustrated above, many patients, previously trained to observe, report that when they engage in worry, they picture something—however vaguely and briefly—connected with the matter of worry and at that moment have tensions as in looking at what they have pictured; or they say something about it to themselves or to others and at that moment have tensions in the speech muscles. So, if they have lost money, they may for a time tend to review pictorially the events connected with their making the investment and an observer may possibly note eye movements and persistent frowning.

Treatment is to be directed toward the voluntary but also the habitual relaxation of tensions specifically accompanying the worrying. That is, if you are such a worrier, you are to learn to relax the eyes so as not to review visual impressions of the events connected with your making the investment. There is some clinical evidence that this can be done to a moderate extent without your closing your eyes, even while you continue to engage in daily affairs. When instructed to relax such tensions, trained observers report that the process of worry ceases for the moment at least. Such reports are secured even when the physician takes every precaution to avoid hinting that a therapeutic effect will be accomplished. In many instances, in fact, patients apparently do not understand clearly what the method is all about until the cessation of worry dawns upon them at least partially a *fait accompli*.

Observation on worried patients suggests that their moments of concern involve particularly often the knitting of the brows, although this tension occurs commonly in most

persons when they are thinking actively or facing relatively
bright light. It may be of interest for you to note how often
this tension occurs in persons you meet. Darwin considered
tension in this region significant, noting that the animal
which frowns or contracts his brows is meeting difficulty.
Under this assumption, if a worrisome patient reports or
seems to show such tension more or less habitually, he is
drilled particularly in relaxing this region. If you are
such a person, you are to practice relaxing the brow,
as instructed in Chapters 13 and 14. These methods obviously apply no less if worry occurs to a pathological
extent.

We are sometimes told that the only way to find out why
a person is melancholic or has certain fears, habits of worry
or other emotional symptoms is to search his past for
psychic causes. Such assumptions are not part of the approach described in this volume. Rather our method is to
observe what the patient is doing muscularly at the moment when his melancholy, fear, worry or other mental
symptoms are present, and if we can identify particular
patterns of contraction, however slight, we proceed as best
we can to eliminate them. If successful in this elimination,
as judged by objective standards, we find that the symptoms tend to disappear.

If you are a worrier or are slightly inclined to "the
blues," there probably are many issues which concern you
needlessly, perhaps producing sleeplessness for many
hours into the night. It may seem to you that you must find
the answer to some problem in hand or that somehow you
must overcome a certain source of irritation. Perhaps the
issue is:

"To be or not to be—
That is the question!"

The best way that I know to handle morbid states of worry is to *keep in mind the distinction between the issue and the attitude.* You must observe that at such moments your attitude is overtense. If you relax the excess tension present in various muscle groups, you attain a quietude of demeanor, and you are likely to report a lessened interest in the issue. Questions that seemed fundamental, crying for an answer, may still appeal to your intellect but no longer affect your emotions so intensely. With habits of advancing relaxation, you tend to become able to adjust yourself to the living conditions you meet, perhaps not approving those conditions, but nevertheless not permitting them to render you overemotional and unfit. I find, however, that the learner needs to be reminded over and over again, when he becomes engrossed in a troublesome matter, to distinguish between the issue and the attitude.

Enough has been said to illustrate the importance of studying nerve currents in the nervous disorders, particularly if reports are secured from subjects trained to observe their tensions and to relax. These methods can be applied not alone to conditions previously mentioned in this chapter but also to other forms of nervous disorder, including undue exaltation and depression.

On the side of treatment, the results already secured in various disorders by progressive relaxation seem to warrant an extension of the method and of the underlying research. Except in acute cases of nervousness, the results are obtained slowly and are therefore not spectacular. But since they depend upon habits gradually and firmly acquired by the patient, it is not surprising that the improvement attained should have notably endured over a term of years. Most of what has been said in the present chapter arises from observations and interpretations in clinical practice. This is suggestive and important, but not yet a science; laboratory investigations are being conducted on an extensive scale. Available methods now supply objective indications of the patient's progress, since objective confirmation is better than mere opinion of the patient or physician.

19

The Quest for Sleep

In many intimate circles a close second to the topic of operations is how to get to sleep at night. One person counts sheep but complains that he lies awake trying to get the last one over the fence. Another drinks warm milk or a certain well-advertised drink, but finds his thirst rather than his need for sleep assuaged. A third lies awake thinking of the day's affairs, unable to shut off his energies. A fourth reads far into the night but finds Morpheus ever more fickle. A fifth tries golf or some other sport and perhaps exults that he has solved the problem until a series of unsuccessful nights leads him to begin his quest anew. A sixth goes off on a vacation and perhaps sleeps very well until soon after his return to daily duties, when his troubles set in again.

Some relate that no sooner do their heads touch the pillow than their thoughts begin a ceaseless flow; others that they fall asleep readily but within a few hours are again awake. Another asserts that he sleeps the night through, but in the morning his fatigue and the disarranged bed show that he has turned and tossed incessantly. A few come to dread the night, and many fear incapacity through fatigue.

Few dwellers in larger communities follow the maxim "early to bed and early to rise". What with electric lighting, automobiles, motion pictures, radios and other innovations, life after dark has become so attractive that most of the evening hours up to midnight are commonly occupied by some form of amusement—if only talking things over with friends and neighbors.

Various factors can "stir up" the nerves, leading away from restful sleep. Aside from the overstimulation of modern living, yet interwoven therewith, are the cares and anxieties that beset us—and often the "pangs of conscience". Shakespeare has made us familiar with these in his "Uneasy lies the head that wears a crown" and "Macbeth hath murdered sleep". Although the Elizabethans did not play bridge into the early hours, interrupting normal habits of rest, or go to the "movies" until their emotions were aroused sufficiently to drive off sleep, doubtless many of them found sources of overstimulation sufficient unto their day. Some might have sought this in conversation, exciting or unduly prolonged; others might have read into the wee hours of the night, until their eyes were filled with images as are ours after like excess. They must have suffered as we do from certain injuries, diseases and disorders of overstimulating character, leading to pain and distress and, accordingly, through increased nerve and muscle tension, to insomnia. Even the "common cold" can sometimes keep us awake. Sound sleep is also unlikely if one has an itching skin disorder.

If we list other factors tending to disturb sleep, we

should not ignore coffee and tea, which may have this effect on persons susceptible to the influence of caffeine. Fatigue can be so severe, however, as to be painful (for instance, in the legs after prolonged standing), and the pain may hinder the onset of sleep. Under these conditions, according to my clinical experience, a cup of coffee or tea may abolish the distress and lead to restful sleep.

Hunger pangs are not conducive to sleep. This tendency is useful, for the pangs lead the hungry animal to seek food before he becomes too weak. However, unless severe, the pangs may disappear for the time being if the individual rests successfully.

Many persons complain that they cannot sleep when it is too hot or when the atmosphere is stuffy. Residents in torrid climes, however, generally succeed in sleeping each night, while many animals seek caves as a favorite place for rest, regardless of fresh air. Evidently the complainers mentioned do not know how to adapt themselves to their environment. Noises are the bane of the existence of many poor sleepers. In consequence, they often insist on extremely quiet locations for their beds and go to various extremes to avoid disturbance. Their very efforts to improve their state, as we shall see later, create a vicious circle, resulting in insomnia. Similar results are seen in those who wear dark cloths to cover the eyes during rest.

It is certain that sleep is a habit very easily disturbed in those who are given to much intellectual work or reflection. Whatever interrupts sleep one night may lead to a period of awakening on the following night, often approximately at the same time.

Exercise in moderation promotes sleep in a healthy manner, because fatigue products are formed, which lead to the natural consequence. Possibly for invalids massage may act as a substitute. Other measures, such as the taking of warm milk regardless of appetite, prolonged immersion in a warm bath or the use of alcoholic beverages, may promote the onset of sleep on a particular occasion in some individuals, but they are approaches to the problem of insomnia from the wrong angle. This is true also of such devices as going to bed after a bath but leaving the skin somewhat damp, or throwing off the bedclothes to cool off and then pulling them up to become gradually warm once more in an effort to aid relaxation. Such practices tend to become fetishes and in some persons promote the development of neurotic attitudes toward sleep in place of the natural indifference that develops with cultivated relaxation. In a word, they encourage habits of reflection about sleep, while on any particular occasion they owe whatever degree of success they attain more often to suggestive conditioning than to normal habits of going to rest.

In a book on sleep by the present author, an imaginary doctor, described by the critics as a "fussy, fictional character", is asked by his patient, "What prevents sleep?"

"What prevents sleep?" he repeats impressively. "The answer is very simple", with a sidelong glance and, pointing with the stem of his pipe, "You!"

"There you are, lying on your bed at night, fidgeting and fuming and fretting that you can't go to sleep. Doubled-up postures, holding down the bed, disordered bedclothes! Why can't you sleep? Precisely because you fidget and fume and fret, either about your loss of sleep or about some other matters, most often some trouble, real or imaginary. It becomes a vicious circle: your fidgets turn aside sleep and your insomnia leads to more fidgets until the more you think about your insomnia and your other troubles, the more you lose sleep. What is the answer? That's what I'm going to try to tell you. But first I want you to understand more fully just why you lose sleep.

"You say that you *can't* sleep; you believe that you *can't* sleep. But can you prove it? Not at all! The most you can prove is that until a certain moment on any night, you did not fall asleep. In spite of repeated attempts, you failed. What do you mean by 'can't'? If you push against a brick wall with all your weight, you are right in saying, 'I can't push it down'. Your proof would be that the wall is solid and heavy, out of all proportion to your strength; but in the same sense you would not be able to prove that you could not sleep. If these newer views are correct, the reason that you fail to sleep is because some of your muscles are tense when they should not be; and who is responsible for this tensing? Your grandmother, whose features you inherit? Your boss, because he scolded you this morning? No! *You* are responsible! *You* are the person doing it!

"Perhaps you feel like saying that when you are tense, you just can't help it. That is what is called a 'good alibi'! If you want to continue to be tense and need an excuse to do so, all I can say is that *your excuses are excellent.*

"Instead of making excuses, consider the facts. There you lie, failing to sleep, because you are repeatedly shifting or moving about in order to become more comfortable. It is certain that, if your nerves and muscles are intact, when you move an arm in order to change something in bed, you

have the ability *not to do it*. I do not mean that you should
restrain yourself from doing it, for this commonly means
that you hold yourself quiet, which is being tense, not
relaxed. I mean that if you have the ability to bend your
arm, you normally have the ability not to. *Ipso facto*, as the
lawyers say. The fact is that when you move about in bed,
seeking comfort, it is you doing so; nothing compels you.
You are led to do it by your own desires and habits; that is
all.

"Your mistake is that you are ever trying to become
a little more comfortable or to avoid discomfort."

"That is natural", you reply.

"But I am reminded of the lesson of Jesus—the paradox
that only by sacrificing your life can you save it. Only by
sacrificing your comfort for the moment, when you lie
awake—relaxing in the face of discomfort, can you eventually become comfortable and go to sleep. It is your persistent effort to better yourself that results in failure;
your effort is tension.

"You are much the same in your daily living. All day
long you are on a tension to meet your appointments, to
make a good impression or to convince your customers.
This is your effort to better your state, to make yourself
more comfortable in life. You have the habit of being
tense in one or another set of muscles or nerves all day
long, as part of your life plan for accomplishment. You
fail to relax for even one moment of the day. I say to you
that you would stand a better chance to accomplish all
your purposes and with greater ease if you would leave
out some of this continual straining. Learn to be a little
more relaxed, instead."

20

Solving the "Mystery" of Sleep

If what has previously been said is true, the basis for
insomnia inevitably has been laid in our habits of
overtense living. When a physical object goes very fast,
we say that it has momentum, and if the object is heavy
we do not expect a mere touch to slow it down. In the same
way, when a human being habitually speeds the responses
of very many different nerves and muscles and keeps up
this rate with only occasional moderate remissions, hour
after hour during the day, we should naturally expect
something of this speed to continue in his tissues long
into the night.

The question of how to shut off our energies at night
had been largely neglected when, in 1908, I turned to the
subject of relaxation, including sleep. The textbook in
physiology then, and until recently, most in vogue in certain medical schools taught that little was known about
sleep and advocated the theory that it depended upon
conditions of blood pressure.

This and certain other views on sleep current at that

time did not seem supported by the results of my early studies. In 1910 my colleagues and I were testing how strong odor sensations appear to subjects under certain conditions. Upon carefully watching the subjects while they paid attention to the source of smell, we found that they engaged in certain tensions. Obviously, various muscles were contracting as they leaned forward, looked at the source of odor, frowned, wrinkled their foreheads, breathed in the odors jerkily and often spoke unnecessarily. Accordingly, without telling them why, I requested them to "abandon all effort" and I instructed them somewhat in relaxing the observed tensions, so that they might smell and pass judgment with a minimum of exertion. Under these conditions, the subjects evidently at times were on the verge of sleep. One subject repeatedly fell asleep whenever he became sufficiently relaxed. It was a pretty clear demonstration that when a person relaxes far enough, sleep automatically ensues.[1]

A certain personal experience in 1908 also gave opportunity for observation. At that time, like many other students who always carry their work with them, I had a nightly insomnia which persisted for hours. Mental activity continued regardless of the need of rest. Upon seeking to discover what it was physiologically that seemed to keep me awake, I found that I could always identify what felt like muscular tensions somewhere in the body and that when these were eliminated by relaxation, sleep took place. Their elimination was not always a rapid process, particularly at first. But as I studied the muscle tensions

[1] This study was published in 1911 from the Psychological Laboratory at Cornell University.

further, I noted that subjectively I seemed responsible for them and therefore apparently could undo them. This evidently depended upon my carrying relaxation sufficiently far. These personal experiences, while having in no sense the character of scientific evidence, have proved of service in the selection of experiments and in the training of subjects and patients.

What we have now come to know about sleep, thanks to the interesting contributions of many students of special problems both here and abroad, would seem to be entirely in harmony with these early views that sleep is essentially a condition of generally reduced activity. When you go to sleep, you usually select a locality relatively removed from sources that would stimulate your eyes, ears and other organs. Under such favorable conditions you lie down and let your muscles relax. As you fall asleep, your breathing becomes more regular, and the breathing out is relatively prolonged in time. Your pulse tends to become slower; your heart beats less forcefully while your blood pressure falls considerably, perhaps reaching a minimum in one to four hours. Probably some increase in blood goes to your brain. That your tissues become generally less active is seen from the fact that if the breath you exhale is tested you are found to be using less oxygen and giving off more carbon dioxide than when awake. Although Professor Carlson has found that the empty stomach continues its contractions undiminished during sleep, other investigators (studying one subject) have found that after the first hour less juice is secreted by the stomach. Among the chemical increases reported to occur during sleep, especially during the first hour, are those of phosphates and of salt (sodium chloride) in the blood and of carbon dioxide tension in the air within the lungs (alveolar air); but the blood is said to be thinner and marked by a decrease of protein. It has also been said that acid characters in the blood increase during sleep. Some investigators have found an increase in the electrical resistance of the skin in certain regions during sleep, but not all investigators have confirmed this result.

As far back as 1887 W. P. Lombard tapped the tendon under the kneecap and noted that the kick is decreased during sleep. Some later investigators observed no kick at all during sleep, while others, including W. W. Tuttle, found none during deep sleep, but registered slight kicks during light sleep. Our own results agree with those of Tuttle. If sleep is deep, the knee-jerk, like certain other deep reflexes, cannot be aroused, but if it is light and restless the kick or other reflex response may be more or less vigorous. Accordingly, since Professor Anton J. Carlson and I found the knee-jerk greatly diminished or absent in subjects relaxed to the greatest possible extent, although still awake, we concluded that by voluntary relaxation while still awake one may attain a degree of nerve-muscle tension lower than that of light sleep.

Various workers have reported that if you lightly scratch the sole of the foot toward the great toe of the sleeper, the toe bends upward, while the other toes tend to bend downward and to spread out. This response (called the Babinski test) is a well-known test used to determine whether the brain and other nerve paths above the spinal cord are working. During extreme relaxation, whether the subject is awake or asleep, this test perhaps does not apply, because then the toes commonly show no motion at all.

That sleep involves general muscular relaxation was clearly stated in 1913 by Henri Piéron, a noted French investigator. He believed, however, that a person does not fall asleep because of relaxation but because of a certain chemical substance appearing in the blood following bodily activities, especially fatigue. My own observations had previously brought out the importance of relaxation in the onset and maintenance of sleep. In 1918 and subsequent years I often observed patients under treatment (or subjects during experiments) falling asleep as they became relaxed.

These individuals were trained to observe sensations from muscle tensions as described in Chapter 13. Such sensations are sometimes called "proprioceptive sensations" —although this term includes also the sensations from the skin, tendons, internal organs and other parts, which indicate to you the states of your body. We found that proprioceptive sensations are characteristic of wakefulness and that when they are diminished during progressive or sudden relaxation, sleep sets in. We do not know, in fact, that sensations from active muscles interfere more with the onset of sleep than do other sensations, such as those from touch and pressure of bedclothes, for these also are increased during muscular contractions, owing to movements of the skin and perhaps to other factors.

During more recent years this doctrine that the onset and maintenance of sleep depend particularly on the reduction of proprioceptive sensations has been advocated by N. Kleitman, H. M. Johnson and other investigators.

Apart from doctrine, the facts seem to be that as relaxation advances, sensory as well as motor nerve impulses diminish and that at some point sleep sets in.

That this does not necessarily depend upon fatigue has been frequently illustrated in my various studies. (We have been handicapped in attempting to make statements about fatigue because until recently we have had no convenient objective measure of it.) Patients being trained to relax for neurotic conditions other than sleeplessness, who therefore have received no suggestions concerning sleep, have usually fallen asleep during periods of general relaxation, regardless of the presence or absence of fatigue. Frequently such occurrences have been noted while the subject was connected with the electrical recording apparatus.

Here is an illustration of the connection between relaxation and sleep. A trained subject lies on a couch. His blood pressure is being taken at frequent intervals from his left arm, while his right arm is connected to wires leading to the recording system. For ten minutes during this experiment he is requested to clench his right fist continuously. That he is doing so can be readily confirmed upon watching the shadow of the recording instrument wire, which vibrates violently as long as the fist is being clenched. But in spite of the instruction, moments occur when somewhat suddenly the wire becomes quiet, showing that the subject quickly relaxes the muscles of his hand; at such moments he snores. Again, if the operator suddenly hears snoring as he looks upon the photographic screen, he sees the wire become quiet. Thereupon, when the operator tells the subject to resume clenching his fist the wire again vibrates, and the snoring ceases. Although we thus have a means of determining precisely the instant when the subject becomes completely relaxed, we have no such means of determining the precise onset of sleep, because the signs of sleep do not distinguish it sharply from general relaxation.

The onset of sleep, then, can be very abrupt. It is commonly effected, according to my clinical observations, at the moment when the eyes and the speech apparatus relax (approximately) completely. The complete relaxation in these particular parts need not be prolonged, I believe, for more than a brief interval; my conjecture is for not more than half a minute. When some subjects fall asleep, the recording wire continues to show relaxation. In others, after an interval of quiet, it soon shows series of marked vibrations. If at such an instant the subject is awakened by the operator, he reports having been dreaming.

Our findings, then, suggest the correctness of the view generally prevalent that the deepest sleep (the most relaxed sleep) is free or relatively free from dreaming.

Restless sleep is generally considered to be not so refreshing as sleep free from frequent movements. Fifteen thousand measurements were taken on eleven subjects lying in beds, wherein certain movements could be recorded. The investigator, Dr. H. M. Johnson, found that during eight hours' sleep at night the average period free from such recorded movements was but eleven and one-half minutes. Such results, however, do not mean that his subjects were relaxed during the intervals between the movements recorded; for the apparatus was not sufficiently sensitive to measure the slighter forms of muscular rigidity and motion.

According to the same psychologist, healthy sleepers shift from one gross bodily position to another between twenty and forty-five times in the course of a typical night of eight hours. Each of these stirs is separated from its nearest neighbor by at least two and a half minutes. He concluded that such "sleep motility" is normal and serves a useful purpose. His conclusion that moving about is desirable in sleep runs counter to common experience. While shifting may satisfy a need of the moment, I have found every indication and suggestion that the quieter the sleeper, the better his rest. Individuals trained to relax can be observed or measured during restful sleep, revealing that movements of the type observed by Johnson are infrequent or altogether absent over extended periods of time.

While sleep can be defined in terms of relaxation, there are various measures to bring on this state aside from those discussed previously. No more brilliant example can be cited than one shown in the moving-picture demonstration before a world congress of physiologists in Boston in the early thirties. Professor L. Hess, a Swiss scientist, showed a number of cats which had undergone operations in which he had inserted and securely fastened fine wires leading through the skull to certain tiny regions in the brain: the gray matter near the intermediate mass and near the head end of the aqueduct which connects the brain cavities. Following the operations the cats had recovered fully and seemed normal in every way. When he connected the wires protruding from the skull with a source of faint electric current, he could stimulate the particular regions mentioned. Thereupon each cat would quickly find itself a comfortable place and go off to sleep. If he stimulated these regions with a strong current, the cat, while in the act of walking off somewhere, would appear to be suddenly deterred from further action, often falling down at once, as if literally thrown into sleep.

When you see or hear or have other sensations, Hess concluded, you are kept awake; but in his experiments and in various ways under normal conditions, the lines leading up to the brain can be interrupted, whereupon incoming messages dwindle or cease, and so you sleep.

21

How to Sleep Well

When you lie down and close your eyes, your muscles
tend to relax and you are (or should be) on the road
toward sleep. So much has long been evident to students
of the subject, but they have not known what makes you
arrive at your destination. Investigations in this clinic
have led to definite conclusions on this matter, as follows: A certain level of nervous-muscular relaxation needs
to prevail generally over your entire system, if sleep is
to take hold. This level probably varies within certain
limits from person to person and from time to time even in
the same person. As stated previously, certain agencies
tend to raise the level of tension present; for example, in
most persons caffeine in sufficient dosage will do so. Other
agencies, such as barbiturates, tend to lower the tension
level. Fatigue products, following exercise in moderation,
doubtless lower this level in a more natural, healthful
manner.

When the muscles of the eyes and of speech relax sufficiently over a period of perhaps thirty seconds, you are
asleep. Note carefully the wording of the last sentence.

Nothing was said to the effect that such relaxation leads to sleep or that it causes sleep, nor was anything said about the state of the brain when sleep begins. To clarify the subject, compare it with eating. We might correctly say that when food is in your mouth and saliva flows, while you chew and swallow, you are eating. This is a statement of fact, although no mention was made about those conditions leading you to eat or causing you to eat, and nothing was said about the brain, either, although certain portions of white and gray matter must act in precise ways in order for you to eat. In brief, certain conditions in the mouth, as mentioned, characterize the act of eating. Likewise, according to our interpretation, relaxation of the eyes and speech, if attained in appropriate measure for a certain brief time, constitute the fact of being asleep. If they are relaxed in this way, you are asleep; if not, you are awake. While other features are essential to sleep, the ones mentioned appear to be pivotal.

In severe fatigue the level of tension present when sleep begins evidently can be very high; for in this way we can explain how soldiers on the march, nearing exhaustion, may go to sleep yet continue walking. The monotony of the march apparently favors this phenomenon. Many persons have fallen asleep while driving a car over long stretches. I have done so more than once on a clear country road at night, notwithstanding the tensions in my leg engaged with the accelerator pedal, those in my arms engaged with steering and those in my neck upholding my head. This illustrates that sleep can come on even in the presence of a certain degree and spread of tension, but such tension must be relatively unvarying, and there must be monotony. What prevents slumber and keeps us awake is quick changes; we can go to sleep (if fatigue products are sufficient) even under conditions of tension, provided that there is no sudden variation, arising from stimuli either outside or inside us, including our own muscles.

Accordingly, you can fall asleep (1) if sufficiently relaxed or (2) even if tense in certain respects, provided that the tensions are maintained steadily. Sleep setting in under tension, I believe, is generally marked by observable movements and fidgets of the sleeper and by dreams; the sleeper also reports later that the sleep has not been completely restful. In "tense" sleep (so to call it) a freely hanging leg kicks vigorously when tapped with a hammer on the tendon below the patella, but in relaxed sleep the kick is slighter or absent altogether. As you fall asleep, if you have been tense in the preceding hours you may jump or jerk all over your body or in some part of it. This is the sleep start. You should ignore it and relax again to sleep; evidently you have been relaxing well just before it occurred, though poorly during the preceding minutes or hours. Accordingly, the sleep start does not occur at night if you have been fairly relaxed during the previous hours of the day.

In clinical experience, restless sleep follows a variety of conditions, such as continual mental activity during the day, particularly if this involved effort or excitement and if it was prolonged up to the moment of retiring; various sorts of emotional excitement, pleasant or unpleasant; overfatigue; fever; the presence of pain or other distress, including excessive warmth or cold; unaccustomed sudden or intermittent sensory disturbances, such as noises; coffee and certain other stimulants. Relaxed sleep is favored by whatever factors tend to promote differential relaxation during the day's activities as well as by a moderate amount of exercise. Clinical experience also commonly ascribes a certain measure of relaxing effect to prolonged tepid baths before retiring, moderate general massage and light but sufficient diet. Some physicians employ sedative drugs or suggestive methods to induce sleep. As is well known, these common measures generally alleviate insomnia but on the whole prove insufficient to induce sleep in difficult cases. They fail to remove effectually the tensions, which, we submit, commonly underlie sleeplessness.

The nervous patient often seems to be hard to satisfy in his sleeping environment. He makes many adjustments. Upon lying down he shifts this way and that, seeking comfort and perhaps finding it, but generally not for long. Many a sleepless person, I have observed, changes his position every few minutes for hours, but the repeated movements cause continued insomnia. Individuals of this type commonly live their daily lives in a similar manner, seldom quite content with what they have or meet with, ever striving for some end not quite attained and keeping active by day as well as by night (at least in thought) to achieve it. To overcome such tendencies insofar as they hamper sleep it is necessary for the individual to realize that he is not to wait to relax until he first has become comfortable, but rather is to take any position that seems fairly comfortable and then to relax in that position in spite of any subsequent discomfort.

In treatment by relaxation no additional means are used to induce sleep; otherwise, when sleep is achieved, we cannot be certain what has been responsible. Furthermore, it seems better to learn to avoid external aids, in the interest of self-dependence. Those who have become dependent on sedative drugs take longer to learn to relax in natural sleep.

Many years ago doctors awoke to the realization that they had frequently treated chronic constipation by means of cathartics and enemas in vain; indeed in many patients such practices can be actually held responsible for the development of chronic constipation. This is known as the "cathartic habit". Similarly, chronic insomnia can result from taking sedatives habitually. How this comes about is illustrated by a patient under treatment. As a test to see whether it would reduce her blood pressure, she was given a sizable dose (three grains) of sodium amytal three times a day, but she was kept in ignorance of the kind of medicine. Although her pressure was not reduced even after eight days of medication, she complained that she was so sleepy that she rode by her station when on the car and was generally inefficient. A week after she had ceased to take the sedative, she volunteered the information that, strange as it might seem, she no longer was able to fall asleep by day (when she rested) as she had prior to the medication. Here was an instance of insomnia in the making! *The individual who becomes accustomed to aids in relaxation in the form of sedatives becomes less able to relax spontaneously.*

Patients who come to the physician can be separated into two classes: those who have been sleeping little or restlessly for a relatively short period such as a few days or weeks or even months, and those who have so suffered for years. In medical practice the methods of relaxation, in a highly abbreviated form, can be useful in showing an ill person how to rest more quietly at once, but the results may not be lasting unless treatment is continued.

In general, insomnia which has been present for only a brief period will be more likely to yield to treatment, other things fairly equal, than insomnia which has existed for many years. Individuals with severe chronic conditions, always associated with other symptoms of high nerve tension, are often unreasonable in their hopes of effecting a cure very promptly. They fail to understand that what they most require is a prolonged course in nervous reeducation. They do not recall that in learning any new skill, such as playing the piano or speaking a foreign language, excellence is not expected within a few weeks or months. While individuals vary greatly in the speed with which they learn to relax, a disordered condition such as insomnia which has lasted for many years commonly does not yield to treatment in less than one year and frequently requires a considerably longer time. The patient generally notes some improvement during the first month or two, but in the usual case upsetting circumstances occur from time to time, and prolonged treatment is required to render him more nearly free from relapses.

PROGRAM FOR SLEEP

If you have been sleepless and desire to learn to shut off your energies at night through relaxation:

Cultivate habits of relaxation at night and during daily activities as directed in Chapters 13 and 14.

Remember that a tense day is likely to be followed by a tense night.

Practice lying down for an hour near noon and near sundown.

Discontinue sedative medicines gradually as soon as your doctor permits.

Assume a fairly comfortable position, and if discomfort sets in do not shift repeatedly but relax in spite of discomfort.

Remember to keep up your daily drill, or you may lose what gains you have made.

Do not be discouraged by relapses.

Above all, try to develop a complete let-go of the muscles of eyes and speech.

Learn to relax to some extent even in the presence of noises or other disturbances, including moderate distress and pain.

If you have long-standing insomnia, this book may aid appreciably, but you probably need personal instruction by a physician to acquire habits of relaxation.

22

Indigestion and Colitis

Tradition has it that when a man is "bilious" or his
digestion upset, he looks sourly upon the world; that
is, his emotional state to some extent depends upon his
digestive organs. Conversely, it is well known that during a period of intense fear before a battle diarrhea is
common among soldiers. When a dog sees savory food,
digestive juices begin to flow in his mouth and stomach
(Pavlow, 1902); but when a cat sees a strange dog, all
movements in the cat's stomach and intestines cease
abruptly (Cannon, 1902).

During nervous or emotional states in man various parts
of his digestive tract are affected, according to evidence
now to be reviewed. When food leaves the mouth, it passes
through a tube of muscle which promptly contracts just
above the food, thus pushing it down to the stomach.
This tube is called the esophagus, and the upper portion
of it can be contracted at will, as in swallowing; but it is
not possible, simply by determining to perform such an
act, to contract the lower portion of it. Under various conditions the muscle of the esophagus contracts unduly and

more or less continuously all along its course, whereupon the passage of food is delayed. We call this phenomenon spasm, and we speak of the "spastic esophagus".

Mild spasm of this sort is likely to occur when you are overemotional or agitated. This was true of two nervous persons who helped us to study the matter in the laboratory. They learned to swallow a small deflated balloon attached to a very thin, hollow rubber tube. When the balloon had descended sufficiently in the esophagus, it was suspended there by a thread attached to a tooth. The balloon was then slightly inflated and the tube was attached to a recording system, which gave us a written record of the amount of air that passed into and out of the balloon. Under these conditions, if the patient was requested to relax all the muscles of his body as far as he could control them, air passed into the balloon, showing that the muscular walls of the esophagus relaxed also. If, on the other hand, the patient was requested to engage in some form of marked mental activity, such as doing arithmetic, as a rule air promptly left the balloon, showing increased tension in the muscular walls of the esophagus. Even a fly alighting on the nose of a subject was found by another, earlier, investigator to cause increased tension.

Such evidence supports the view that in highly nervous or emotional persons we should expect some measure of spasm of the esophagus to be frequently present. This expectation has been substantially confirmed in X-ray studies which I have made in past years on more than one hundred such patients. Such a study is carried out by having the patient take a single swallow of barium paste, which, as previously mentioned, is opaque to X-rays and therefore can be readily identified by the dark shadow it produces. In the normal students tested, all the paste passed through the esophagus in about one minute or less, but in nervous patients there generally is considerable delay, which in severe conditions may exceed an hour. Such delay indicates some degree of spasm.

It is well known that there are many causes of spasm of the esophagus besides nervous or emotional states. Among such causes are ulcer of the stomach, acute appendicitis and other irritating conditions. A long list of these has been compiled by a doctor interested chiefly in organic derangements. Accordingly, before we conclude that the spasm found in any individual is due merely to overactive nerves, a careful examination must be made to determine whether the patient is free from any local source of irritation, such as an inflammation or a tumor. It is important that the individual who suspects that he has spasm should consult his physician, because his discomfort may be caused by an ulcer or even by cancer.

If nervous overactivity is as widespread as many believe and if this tends to be reflected in spasm of the esophagus, we need not be surprised that, according to Dr. Clyde Brooks, spasm of the esophagus is the most common of all the ailments of the digestive tract. The symptoms vary somewhat and do not always include difficulty in swallowing to a degree noticeable by the patient. Most typically, in the moderate or incipient conditions, which predominate in number over the severe types and to which our discussion is limited, the patient mentions a "lump in the throat" or "choking sensation" or "a feeling of tightness or pressure" usually somewhere in the front portion of the chest or upper part of the abdomen, but sometimes passing to the back. At times there may be a dull ache or even intense pangs of pain. The sensation is not generally relieved, except for a brief period, by the taking of food or by alkaline powders and not altogether by moving the bowels. Belching of air may be frequent in such conditions and usually brings partial temporary relief. Sometimes the patient swallows air but does not know it and does not know how to stop it; there result distress and a feeling of fullness in the upper part of the abdomen. The distress generally does not occur at any particular period of the day; nevertheless its peculiar character and location often lead the doctor to suspect ulcer of the stomach or duodenum, and he must use great caution to avoid mistakes.

One of the persons who aided in the studies above mentioned was a nineteen-year-old university student. When first seen in January, 1923, he complained of a severe cramping or burning pain in the upper part of the abdomen, which had been continuous for hours each day during the previous three years. Under the X-ray, his duodenum did not seem quite normal; there appeared to be a slight fleck or scar, as if he had once had an ulcer there. He frequently experienced a feeling of fright which he could not distinguish from the pain. This appeared particularly when he was under nervous strain, such as when he recited in class or when he was present at large gatherings or in the company of the other sex. He mentioned also frequent feelings of irritability and difficulty in concentration.

Neither our aims here nor the space available permit us to give a detailed account of the condition of this individual or of his progress as he learned to relax. This has been done sufficiently in another place (*Progressive Relaxation*, 1938). But some of the chief points in his history are interesting to recall. About three weeks after the onset of his pain, he had lost ten pounds and had become somewhat weak. A few months later he was examined by a competent internist, who, because of a certain apparent relation of the distress to mealtimes, at first suspected that the patient had an ulcer of the duodenum. But after many careful examinations it was decided that probably there was no active ulcer. Accordingly, a year or so later he was sent to a neurologist, who talked to him severely and succeeded in curing him of certain fears directed toward women; but he was left with other fears and with the severe pain.

Our studies, made with the aid of the balloon as well as the X-ray methods, indicated that when he was fearful and in pain simultaneous evidences of contraction in the various muscles of his body could be readily observed. As he learned to relax these muscles, the symptoms he complained of seemed to decrease accordingly. Individual tests by the balloon and X-ray methods revealed that during a period of pain and distress, accompanied, as said above, by visible muscle tensions, the instruction to relax those tensions was followed by a prompt or gradually progressive relaxation of the esophagus, with relief from distress as long as the relaxation was maintained. The period of treatment required was unusually long, but in approximately two years, he stated that he was usually free from pain. Since then, when relapses have occurred, they have appeared to the patient as well as to the physician to be due to failure to keep up his practice and to apply what he learned. While on the whole he has made headway against his earlier habits of overactive nerves and while he has become better balanced emotionally, he has had to contend with a singularly sensitive digestive tract and some years ago suffered from a hemorrhage, presumably from the duodenum. Under these conditions it became necessary to supplement the treatment with nonirritating diet and medication. Since he complained that whenever pain recurred he noticed that he had been in a tense state previously, it has seemed best to continue to coach him in advanced techniques of relaxation. As a rule he generally appears more relaxed.

Our studies, then, support the view that the esophagus is active in emotional states and that it is part of the mechanism involved in your adjustment to your daily affairs. When you meet difficulties, and particularly if you are seldom free from them, the esophagus varies in its tensions from moment to moment, but on the whole an increase in tension is characteristic; and so we may say that the esophagus is frequently somewhat spastic. The symptoms may be slight, or they may trouble you to such an extent that you consult a doctor. The evidence suggests that the symptoms from the esophagus depend for their presence upon tensions in the outer, or skeletal, muscles and can be controlled if the individual learns to relax these muscles. The methods for this relaxation have already been given in earlier chapters. It should be emphasized that a mere superficial carrying out of such directions should not be expected to effect such control if marked pain is present. In any event persons with painful conditions should be in charge of their physician.

Much of what has been said concerning the esophagus would seem to apply also to the large intestine or colon. This organ, like the esophagus and other sections of the digestive tract, is a hollow, tubelike structure, the walls of which in a healthy person are composed mostly of muscle. Although variations in chronic overtenseness or spasticity in the esophagus doubtless are not always accompanied by similar variations in the colon, it has seemed in my experience to be generally true that the person with a more or less spastic colon has also a tendency toward spastic esophagus and vice versa. We are led to suspect that constipation, so prevalent in this country and in so many cases associated with spastic colon, is due in large measure to the overactive nervous lives we lead.

When the doctor tells you that you have "colitis" but that he has failed to find any bacteria or amoeba or any inflammation or other local irritation, he is likely to add that he believes that your bowel symptoms are due to your nervous tendencies. Perhaps there have been frequent bowel movements or diarrhea, with air passing often by rectum; or perhaps there have been thin, firm stools shaped like ribbons or like cigarettes. Inspection from time to time may disclose mucus, whereupon the condition is termed "mucous colitis". Abdominal pain in many instances is severe and cramplike before the bowels move and at other times. The distress as well as the diarrhea or constipation may become particularly marked on divers occasions such as after partaking of certain foods which seem to disagree with you or after unusual physical exertion or after contracting a cold, but they are particularly characteristic following periods of nervous and mental strain. Under the X-ray, if a meal including barium has been taken eight to twenty hours previously, the colon is seen irregularly narrowed in its various parts, sometimes almost to the point of being completely closed. In chronic cases of long standing a certain smooth and distended appearance of the colon suggests to the experienced eye that the intestinal muscle has become somewhat reduced and atrophied, presumably due to years of spasticity.

In chronic nervous colitis correct diagnosis is particularly important because of the danger of unnecessary operations. This danger arises because in this condition tenderness in the region of the appendix or gall-bladder is often found and can be mistaken for inflammation requiring surgery. Rollin T. Woodyatt (1927) cites such a case, in which an operation was almost performed after a severe colonic spasm was revealed by the Roentgen ray. Fortunately, later films proved negative, and the operation was avoided. But when tenderness is found near the gall-bladder or the appendix or both, as often occurs in this common malady, who can say how many futile operations are performed for this condition each yea : my own experience, as previously said, suggests that there are many. Evarts Graham in his surgical address at the opening of the Medical School of the University of Chicago also warned against this error.

An interesting illustration may be briefly recounted, again referring to *Progressive Relaxation* for details. Mrs. E. T., fifty-eight years old, a member of a notable Irish family, complained in January, 1922, that for the past thirty years she had been subject to attacks of mucous colitis. They had increased in frequency until now they had appeared two or three times a month. They were increasing in severity also, for pain had been marked during the last four years all over the abdomen, sometimes shooting down the thighs, sometimes passing with a burning sensation up under the sternum. These attacks generally lasted for about two days, and the pain could be relieved only by an electric pad and by a dose of baking soda. Cramping abdominal pain occurred with any bowel movement, and distress in the upper part of the abdomen appeared usually within five to ten minutes after eating or drinking. This pain generally disappeared spontaneously an hour or two after eating. At times she was constipated and often weak, she said, and unable to engage in normal activities.

The examining hand found the colon firm along its entire course and tender particularly near the regions of the gall-bladder and the appendix. In the X-ray film a highly spastic colon was revealed, so narrowed near the spleen that it appeared like a stricture. This was no cancer, for the colon filled out when an enema containing barium was given. Although previous treatment through restriction of diet and the use of various medicines had failed to effect lasting improvement, for several months I also attempted to relieve the condition through these measures. I had not previously applied progressive relaxation to chronic colitis, and, oddly enough, in this case it was the consulting surgeon who suggested that progressive relaxation be tried.

Treatment by progressive relaxation was accordingly begun in May, 1922. The study was of additional interest because other measures, including diet and rest, had been carefully employed without satisfactory effect. This patient was not very apt at learning to recognize muscular contractions. Among the striking tensions outwardly revealed was a persistent severe frown and a frequently wrinkled forehead. Much practice was devoted to relaxing these regions. During the following months as she became relaxed in these and other parts, the hospital records showed a gradual disappearance of mucus from the stools. By August, 1922, when the patient was still in the hospital, the gall-bladder region had become entirely free from tenderness, and pain had become diminished or absent. The stools as a rule had become normal.

At home the patient continued without further medical aid to improve at relaxing her muscles, just as an individual will improve with practice after instruction in piano playing or dancing or other physical skills. After about six months more the tenderness had disappeared from the abdomen completely. She went to California, nursed her husband, who had become ill, swam and drove a motorcar with impunity for the first time in many years. An X-ray film kindly made for me in 1925 by Dr. A. B. Smith at La Jolla revealed a colon no longer extremely spastic. Colonic pain was absent excepting after housework, which she therefore avoided. In 1927 she stated that her general condition had been highly satisfactory for five years with only slight relapses. She continued to practice relaxation regularly, particularly if she felt any difficulties coming on. In 1930, when last I saw her, frowning seemed very greatly diminished. She had had no recurrences, was on full diet and appeared very well.

Striking as are these results, six months of treatment is considered insufficient to eradicate habitual colonic spasm in patients so ill. As education in the field of relaxation progresses, it is to be hoped that people will seek more than increased comfort and the abatement of symptoms. Maladies entrenched for years in unhealthful nervous habits should be treated thoroughly by these newer methods until results are attained securely, as judged by objective standards.

Patients differ greatly in the degree of skill they acquire in continuing habits of relaxation they have learned. Some, neglecting practice, tend to retrogress, but even with these I am inclined to believe that relaxation once well learned is, like swimming, more or less a permanent possession. I have seen instances where, in spite of reported faithful practice, retrogression has occurred, at least for a time; but the rule, on the whole, has seemed to be in the direction of the adage that practice makes perfect.

Of late years more than twenty cases of marked spastic or mucous colitis have been treated by relaxation alone, with the patient on full diet practically from the outset; and if we consider only those cases in which treatment and practice were regularly maintained for a year or more as directed by the physician, the results have been in most cases a gradual abatement of symptoms and resumption of normal vigor.

In addition to actual colitis, we should mention the spells of abdominal symptoms frequent in many nervous persons, which are like those seen in outright cases of spastic colitis except that they are not so severe; the course of these evidently could be controlled by the introduction of relaxation and recurrence probably prevented.

In 1929 experience in the treatment of ulcer of the stomach and duodenum prompted me to suggest that these maladies might be of nervous origin and that physicians might very well investigate whether they would not subside in patients trained to relax. Careful investigation was extremely difficult because of the frequent necessity of medication and diet. Prior to this suggestion, it had been generally believed that infection played a primary role in the causation of such ulcers. However, following my suggestion, the view became widely prevalent among physicians that peptic ulcer arises in nervous people. While impressed with the agreement of clinicians on this point, I admitted in earlier editions of this volume that scientific investigations remained to be made. (See also pages 39 and 40.)

In résumé, I have proved, at least in the several persons studied, that during marked emotion various parts of the digestive tract take part, becoming increasingly tense or spastic. If nerves are chronically overactive, various symptoms may arise from the parts of the digestive tract most affected. In these conditions tenderness in particular regions should not be mistaken for severe inflammation requiring surgery. The evidence to date indicates that the common cases of spastic portions of the digestive tract may be favorably treated through relaxation.

In chronic colitis and in peptic ulcer, if your doctor has advised relaxation:

Practice lying down at least one-half hour before each
meal.

Watch for frowning or other habitual tensions and eliminate these.

Be sure to learn to relax your abdominal muscles.

Make differential relaxation a habit during your daily affairs.

23

What Causes High Blood Pressure

During the past two decades, evidence has been accumulating concerning what can be done for patients with high blood pressure by methods of progressive relaxation employed either alone or with the aid of accessory methods including medication and diet. Slowly I have come to the conclusion that if treatment is begun sufficiently early in the course of the disease, there often is the possibility of very great improvement, amounting approximately even to cure.

Chronic high blood pressure can be due to various causes, including kidney, heart and glandular disease, but in about ninety per cent of the instances seen among our populace no such underlying malady is present. Since the cause has not been known, doctors have called the common variety "essential hypertension". In the early stages of this disorder, the blood pressure is elevated from time to time at least, but as yet little or no marked changes are demonstrable in the heart, kidneys or eye-grounds. Accordingly, in a former report I announced that the results in seventeen patients with early essential hypertension indicated that the disorder could be arrested in its progress and that the individual could learn to live in health. I quote from this report.[1]

"With the discovery of insulin, the sulfa drugs, penicillin and other molds, Medicine reached a new peak of achievement; but there has been no such triumph over the cardiovascular diseases which rank as Public Killer #1. Why? Are we failing because we cling to the weapons which won the last war? Perhaps students a century hence will look back upon an epoch which inclined to treat man as little more than a combination of chemicals.

"He is that, to be sure, and therefore chemical analysis is necessary. He has a body and therefore surgery and other physical procedures often can remove diseased parts, or mold and ply them. But my thesis today is that he is more than a mass of physical cells composed of chemical substances. He is more than a mind attached to a body to be probed and analyzed by psychiatrists of different schools of thought. He is a self-directing individual.

"As such, he directs the distribution and expenditure of his own energies in what has been called the struggle for existence, or better said, the effort to get ahead. This is possible only through the contraction of muscle fibers. Mobility and the power to exert force on external bodies resides in muscle tissue alone of all tissues. Here is a fact which I believe has been underestimated in trying to understand the development of high blood pressure.

"That excitement and emotion tend to raise blood pressure, especially in persons predisposed to high tension, has

[1] The address was at a meeting of the American Association for the Advancement of Science in Chicago, and was entitled "On the Control of Blood Pressure in Man".

not been overlooked. On the contrary, doctors know it well and investigators have confirmed it in numerous laboratories. I have not come here today merely to rehash this well-known fact, but to add other facts not so well known. During states of emotion or excitement, men and women studied in this Laboratory have shown tense muscles; action-potentials in various voluntary muscles have been high as compared with control tests on the same person when not excited or emotional.

"That blood pressure often increases during emotion we confirm once more. But in addition we find that in the presence of effort, even without excitement and intense emotion, general muscular tension can increase as much as it does during emotional excitement. Likewise the increase of blood pressure may be as great as that seen during emotional excitement. After fifteen years of study of this particular subject in this Laboratory, it seems clear that tenseness all over the body commonly occurs not only with emotions and nervous excitement, but also during states of effort when these conditions are absent. Daily life is in fact a succession of complex muscular acts consisting of efforts and what might be called subefforts, when the actions are so slight as to require delicate instruments to detect and measure them."

But all our efforts depend upon our blood pressure and when they increase, the blood pressure tends to be increased accordingly. This occurs reflexly. For efforts are muscular contraction, which is a fire or combustion in muscle. The supplies of fuel (blood sugar) and of oxygen must come from the blood and so the heart pumps harder and the arterioles contract further to increase the blood pressure so as to furnish the supplies needed for our efforts. Also when combustion is increased, like the fire in your hearth, there is more ash which has to be carried away. When efforts are increased, there are increased waste products, including minerals which are cast off—lactic acid, pyruvic acid and other end-products. To carry off these excess products, the blood has an increased job. This is accomplished by mechanisms which increase the blood pressure, including increased pumping force of the heart as well as tensing of the walls of arteries of very small types. The story is similar if the individual has to flee from trouble. Certain tissues then have greater need for supplies, while at the same time what corresponds to ashes in a fireplace must be carried off. Once more there is need of elevated blood pressure.

If the need of active muscles for an increased blood supply is not satisfied, fatigue sets in quickly. When fatigue is felt as a sensation, this is nature's signal to the individual to go more slowly or to quit; in our terms, it is a signal to relax. This can be illustrated in a simple experiment, in which a tourniquet or a blood pressure cuff is fastened tightly about the upper arm while the individual pulls against weights with the same hand. The tighter the bandage the less the blood supply and in consequence the sooner and more severe the resultant fatigue.

In a sense, the lives of many men and women are more or less a continuous struggle. Much of the time, as said previously, their energies are engaged in efforts to meet and overcome difficulties. Thereupon the blood pressure increases until in many instances, as a result of unremitting efforts, it becomes chronically high.

Without doubt you know of many persons who lead a strenuous life of the sort described yet who never develop high blood pressure. Why? We cannot yet answer this question fully. However, light on the answer to the problem is beginning to be shed from numerous sources. I quote again from the report:

"The investigations of Goldblatt and numerous others render indubitable that there are instances in which hypertension results from anemia of the kidney, but up to date there has been no conclusive evidence that this is the chief cause in the common malady known as essential hypertension. Among certain physiologists there has recently been a swing toward the opposite direction, for the view has gained ground that the nervous system may be primarily responsible. Studies which have encouraged this view have been those made on Norway rats, which have been rendered lastingly hypertensive by sand blasts blown past their ears. In these instances, the origin doubtless lies in the nervous system and not in the kidney. We must await further evidence as to man. The results which I shall report do not rule out the importance of anemia of the kidney, but they suggest that essential hypertension in man results from overactivity of the nervous system in individuals who are somehow organically susceptible to this disorder.

"Evidence that the tendency to develop hypertension is probably hereditary has been advanced by Ayman. Whether this tendency resides primarily in the blood vessels, the kidney, in the nervous system or all together remains to be determined. *We do not yet know but that anybody, if driven far enough by the exigencies and trials of life, may develop high blood pressure.*"

24

How to Reduce High Blood Pressure

Anybody with high blood pressure should be under the care of a doctor interested in the field. Self-treatment is not to be encouraged. However, doctors commonly agree that persons with high blood pressure should learn to relax.

The role of scientific relaxation was recently shown in a scientific exhibit before the Chicago Medical Society prepared for the medical profession by the Foundation for Scientific Relaxation, Incorporated not-for-profit. It was entitled "The Tension in Hypertension". I shall tell of this in lay terms in the first portion of this chapter.

The Germans name the common form of hypertension "hypertonia". To them as to us it is one of the great plagues of the present day. The name which they employ calls attention to the excessive tension we know to ·be present in the little circular muscles in the walls of the small arteries or arterioles. In addition, however, we know also that when this disease advances, the heart muscle increases, evidently from overuse. In my view, chronic high blood pressure means increase of the central pump action from the very first day.

In other words, it would appear that high blood pressure (essential hypertension) involves increased tension in the muscles of the heart and of the small blood vessels at least.

Certain persons, we believe, are by heredity rendered more susceptible to developing this disease. What they lack we can only guess; perhaps the elastic tissue in their arteries is poor; perhaps the nerve supply to their vessels or the glandular system is hyperirritable; perhaps there is some other defect. In any event, how these people perform under strains and "stresses" of present-day environment must depend upon the tissues in their blood vessels; just as must the performance of any man-made instrument like an automobile depend upon the quality of the materials and their useful arrangement in the structure thereof.

This view seems supported by common sense. If your car breaks down under stresses and strains of modern driving, we can conclude that it is a "lemon", poorly manufactured; but in many a breakdown, including those resulting from collisions, it is impossible to gauge to what extent the fault lay in poor driving and care of the car or from structural defects.

Experience with patients in the early states of chronic high blood pressure suggests that there may be little wrong with them pathologically; that even if the tissues inherited by individuals are normal, they may live so tensely as to develop chronic essential hypertension nevertheless.

Living tensely, as shown in early chapters, is to engage

in excessive efforts for success of one kind or another. There is chronic excess of tension in the muscles which perform in our each and every effort of daily life.

This constitutes a chronic excessive demand for action by the circulatory system. It is as simple as that. The person who gets high blood pressure as a rule "asks for it".

How does this demand work out? Each pattern of muscle effort occurs only through the cooperation of the circulatory system. For muscle contraction is combustion, which requires fuel and oxygen. The supply of blood sugar and oxygen is brought by the blood, since muscle contraction stimulates the process by reflex routes. But combustion in muscle also results in waste products, including mineral ash. These products must be transported from the muscle for disposal elsewhere.

Thus each and every muscle contraction (the essential ingredient in our waking efforts) is a reflex demand on the circulatory system. This results not only in increased movement of blood to and from the contracting muscle; at least as important as movement of the blood is its pressure. Much or most of the work of the heart is required to maintain or increase blood pressure.

Thus with every effort, with or without emotion, there is variable increased demand for blood pressure elevation. This effect is exaggerated in persons with tendencies toward high blood pressure.

In them and in healthy persons this effect applies as much to so-called mental as to physical activities. For my laboratory studies have shown that in each and every mental act, a specific neuromuscular pattern can be identified by sensitive electrical measurements.

The exhibit included X-ray films of the esophagus, stomach and colon characteristically found in patients with essential hypertension. The muscles of these viscera rendered them "spastic". The patients commonly show corresponding symptoms: constipation, "gas"; belching; and spells of abdominal pain. When these symptoms become aggravated, these patients commonly believe that they have some "new" disease of the digestive organs. As a rule this is not true, for the spastic digestive tract is part and parcel of the total disease.

Accordingly, we see that tension characterizes the common form of chronic high blood pressure known as essential hypertension. The tension is excessive in all of the muscles of the body, including those of the blood vessels and other visceral organs.

According to the facts and views presented, most cases of high blood pressure result from excessive effortful response to the pressures of everyday life, especially in those with poor hereditary structure.

What are persons to do who have this condition? Very often they resort to certain drugs.

In recent years extracts of snake-root have been introduced for lowering blood pressure. The site of action of these extracts is perhaps in a section of the brain (the hypothalamus) or adjacent thereto. Possibly, however, the action is to diminish certain blood pressure raising substances naturally present in certain nerve cells (ephedrine and norephedrine). We are not yet certain. Other compounds, known as "ganglionic blockaders," also have come into common use, and there are still others.

These drugs are easy for the doctor to prescribe and for

the patient to take; but admittedly they fail to get at the basic cause, as demonstrated in the exhibit. They diminish our efforts to achieve success, but not in a natural, healthy manner. Most of them fail to reduce blood pressure much in the lying posture, which points to the defective action of these particular drugs.

What they do, insofar as they succeed at all, is mostly to act as mild toxins; in lay terms, they poison some section of our effort-circuits and thus throw this circuit partially out of action. Except in large doses, they often fail to lower the pressure to the extent that scientific relaxation can accomplish. And scientific relaxation tends to lower pressure as much in the lying position as in any other. Obviously this is accomplished without the toxic action upon which drug administration largely depends.

These drugs often produce toxic side-effects, troublesome to patient and to doctor. Often they fail to reduce the blood pressure lastingly, for the effects of any medicine tend to wear off in time. On the other hand, scientific relaxation tends to produce more lasting effects, provided that the patient keeps up his daily practice.

Another disadvantage of the drugs is that they often tend to render the patient drowsy, diminishing his alertness and drive.

Scientific relaxation, however, does not render the patient drowsy and, if anything, tends to increase his drive markedly. It frees him from inhibitions, averts fatigue, conserves his energies and thus promotes daily efficiency.

Physiological relaxation is applicable to the basic needs of the patient prone to hypertension. It is not to be confused with hobbies, recreation, golf or other exercise (however beneficial or not). Rather it is a highly technical field, like ophthalmology, not to be learned from books, but only under competent instructors.

It is as harmless as breathing. There are no objectionable features, like the side-effects from hypotensive drugs. A skilled person, normal or hypertensive, can lower his blood pressure by technical muscular relaxation within a few minutes. Thus he can learn by differential relaxation to attain increased work performance but with less muscular energy expenditure in his daily living. When his muscles become trained to be less demanding, his blood pressure drops automatically.

Accordingly we are led to regard physiological living as a muscular art which can be learned to advantage by anyone, whether normotensive or hypertensive. The individual learns to take the "stresses" and "strains" of daily life in a relaxed stride. If pathological changes are not too far advanced, and if the pressure seems moderated, the trained hypertensive is permitted a full life of vigorous work and play without any restriction.

The hypertensive cannot be cured if this means giving him a new set of arteries free from sclerosis and a new heart. But a follow-up over the years of some patients who received thorough training for severe hypertension shows persistent values around normal values most of the time along with apparently restored health. Among these have been business executives and others who have worked hard.

Our results bear on the etiology as well as on the management of essential hypertension. They afford evidence that whatever the inherited tendencies toward pathological change in arterioles, if any, usage determines the wear and tear. And usage means how tensely the individual lives.

Accordingly the conservation of the patient's arteries leads us to promote the conservation of his muscular energies. Thus for various reasons scientific relaxation, where available, is evidently the method of choice for the lasting reduction of high blood pressure. However, in severe cases, the hypotensive drugs can be used in addition. The hope is to use them only temporarily, however, as a crutch. In the course of months, when the patient has learned to relax, the aim is to discard them as soon as the blood pressure becomes habitually reduced.

What is the upper limit of blood pressure values in cases which have responded favorably to scientific relaxation methods? I can cite two dramatic instances: a housewife of about forty. Before treatment, her systolic pressure reached 252, while her diastolic pressure was 140. A man of about thirty-eight, married, with five children. He had been a pilot, working for an airline. Before treatment, his systolic pressure reached 260, while his diastolic pressure was 160. Both patients received daily doses of the drugs mentioned until they had become proficient at scientific relaxation. Both became skilled at relaxing during their daily occupations while they believed their efficiency at their tasks was increased.

After the medicine could be stopped, it was evident that each had attained high skill. Three months after the medicine was stopped, the housewife mentioned on one occasion showed a systolic pressure of 97, while the diastolic value was but 72. This sort of dramatic result has almost been equalled by the captain, but his technique is not quite so good.

There are other approaches deserving of mention. Among these is surgical removal of much of the sympathetic nervous system. This should be reserved, I believe, for some very severe cases with advanced hardening of the arteries of the retina and the kidney.

As doctors long have known, blood pressure tends to fall with weight reduction. Therefore, it has been common practice to reduce the weight of obese persons suffering from high blood pressure. However, most doctors refrain from reducing the weight of patients who are not obese, for fear of weakening them. There are many patients who are not overnourished, but have high pressure. It has proved possible to reduce blood pressure effectively even without weight reduction or other measures with methods of progressive relaxation.

The rice diet has attracted less attention of late. Indeed, we know of no special virtue inherent in rice for the reduction of blood pressure. In the rice diet as commonly prescribed, the salt intake is low. By salt is meant sodium chloride. Most people eat about eight grams of salt per day, or more, but the body actually does not require so much. About two grams are sufficient for bodily needs. We salt our food because we like to, but added salt is not absolutely necessary. Many foods contain large quantities of salt, even when no extra salt is added by the cook or by ourselves at the table. An example is celery, which is rich in salt. Even when the attempt is made to exclude salt in so-called salt-free bread, a relatively large amount of salt can sometimes be precipitated upon analysis. I found this to be true when I introduced what is now called "salt-free diet". This was during studies on peptic ulcer, as reported in the *Journal of the American Medical Association* in 1917.

Any reducing diet, then, including the rice diet, may diminish blood pressure in some patients at least temporarily. In addition, the rice and other forms of diet low in salt doubtless will tend to reduce pressure in those who suffer from salt retention. To this extent various types of diets can prove useful, including the rice diet. However, in the light of what has been said, it is doubtful that the rice diet really solves the common problem of blood pressure.

Where relaxation can be employed in the treatment of high blood pressure, the advantages are clear:

1. There is no risk as in surgery, and there is no pain and in all events no harm.
2. In early but also in moderately advanced cases, the individual is permitted to remain at his work. Commonly he devotes one hour per day to practice, preferably at noon. If he can find two hours, the second perhaps at eventide, so much the better.
3. If the foregoing theory is sound, as the general physiology of the subject would lead us to believe, then in cases to which it applies, progressive relaxation is not only an empirical but also a rational approach; it tends to do away with one important common cause of high blood pressure.
4. Because it lessens the amount of daily work required of the heart, relaxative treatment tends to diminish

heart strain in the popular sense of the word. Here we should think of differential as well as of general relaxation.

5. The effects of this therapy are favorable for the general health, tending to build up reserves.

6. It can be combined with medication, with diet and even with surgery. Indeed I would emphasize the usefulness of training to relax as a preparation for surgery. In addition, some patients find it useful, even necessary, to learn to relax following operation. This is not only because operation fails to reduce pressure in some instances. I well recall the example of one young practicing physician who came to my clinic to learn to relax after he had been operated upon. After taking his pressure carefully, I turned to him a little gruffly and said, "Doctor, your pressure is normal! What are you doing here?" He replied with prompt good humor, "That's why I came. I want to keep it so!"

When blood pressure can be reduced sufficiently by relaxation methods *alone*, the advantages of this simple and effective treatment are clear. The individual can enjoy regular full diet and is even permitted to drink and smoke in moderation. He continues at his usual duties, both business and social. Such freedom from restrictions is more likely to be accorded in instances where tests show that the arteries have not suffered too much change and that the kidney and heart functions are good. Obviously in such matters decision must be made as applied to each individual.

The minds of individuals with high blood pressure are

not at rest. They imagine what they should be doing, recall what they have done and reflect about things too much: sometimes the play of emotions is almost incessant. It is a popular fallacy that as a rule worry is solely responsible when nervousness and excitement raise blood pressure. On the contrary, daily measurements of pressure in my laboratory afford convincing evidence that pressure rises likewise with gaiety and pleasant experiences of all types. Even when the issue involved is trivial, suspense often seems to raise the diastolic pressure.

Without doubt, then, many persons with overactive minds develop hypertension while others with the same overactivity do not. We explain this under the assumption that there must be an organic predisposition to this malady if it is to develop. As said previously, evidence suggests that this predisposition can be inherited. If the mind is really overactive in most instances of essential hypertension, it is especially important to learn how to relax the tensions present during mental activities.

Careful investigation requires that we ourselves raise possible objections to our own views. In the present instance we might question whether training to relax is really effective in lowering the blood pressure or whether merely taking a rest or nap each day might not bring equally good results. A case in point is a sixty-year-old surgeon in a special field, who presented himself for treatment by the method of relaxation but who said that he had rested daily for eighteen months previously. Not alone had daily rests without training to relax failed to reduce his pressure, but he had not succeeded in acquiring habits of muscular relaxation when he lay down to rest. Electrical measurements disclosed that his arms and other parts continued to be in a tense state, the reverse of relaxation, and that he failed to rest properly. Upon his learning to relax, his blood pressure has become more nearly normal, although he has continued to work hard in his profession. Other instances of this sort have furnished evidence that training to relax is significant and is not to be replaced by daily rests alone.

The doctor mentioned had previously put himself on a reducing diet and had lost thirty-five pounds, bringing himself down to his proper weight. Nevertheless, this measure, added to the daily rests, had failed to reduce his pressure. Only when he learned to relax was lasting reduction brought about.

Concerning the cause of high blood pressure, one finding in this Clinic has always seemed to me surprising. This is the need of making relaxation technically complete in order to attain the most marked reduction of blood pressure. If relaxation is incomplete and residual tension is present (even to the extent of merely a millionth of a volt, as measured in wires in the muscle under test), the blood pressure of the patient may fail to fall markedly. This apparently explains why daily rests without training commonly fail. How so slight a residue can be responsible for so overwhelming a result is still not fully explained. But the fact remains and must be reckoned with if treatment is to be effective.

What can be accomplished by technical relaxation alone is illustrated in the instance of one prominent man who feared that he might have to resign from his very important position because of high blood pressure. He was fifty-nine years old and had been informed of the first signs of increased pressure eighteen years previously. His condition had been investigated with care and skill at two great medical institutions, but no effective treatment had been available. However, when he learned to relax week by week and month by month, his pressure for most of the time dropped to normal and remained there (with occasional relapses). He was discharged in an improved nervous state. Treatment was by relaxation alone. At seventy-six, he considered himself well and displayed unusual vigor in keeping himself employed. He lived to be eighty-four.

Headache and dizziness often accompany high blood pressure. In most instances these symptoms diminish or disappear early in the course of treatment by the method of relaxation, sometimes even before the pressure is markedly reduced. This resembles effects often seen after an operation but is the reverse of what sometimes occurs after the taking of medicines, in which case the distress and discomfort often persist. Sedatives have lost their former popularity among many leading physicians because reductions generally have failed to persist. Likewise, special diets which include the avoidance of red meats no longer have their former vogue. While sources of infection should be located and removed in any patient, however healthy otherwise, the view has lost ground that the cause of high blood pressure generally can be removed thereby.

The reduction of pressure, both systolic and diastolic, may require many months, or may begin to appear as early as the first week. Occasionally I have seen this even in advanced cases and even where there was a history of

hypertension in the patient's family. However, as far as I
know, one result is occasionally seen following relaxation
but no other form of treatment. Some of the patients
whose pressure has been lowered to normal levels show at
times readings definitely below normal. For example, a
patient in the fifties, whose earlier pressures were as high
as 180 or more systolic and 130 diastolic, after about six
months' training entered the office with a pressure reading
systolic 115 and diastolic 84. She felt well and vigorous.
That this can occur once more suggests that the relaxation
method probably removes an essential part of the cause in
at least some conditions of high blood pressure.

In treatment by the doctor not fewer than 100 periods
of instruction are advised. Obviously, the better the training, the less the danger of relapse, and the better prepared
is the patient to meet the strains and hardships which
expectedly or unexpectedly arise to disturb the even tenor
of his life. Certain patients who have had a relatively small
number of treatments during a period of months, finding
themselves restored to health, including normal pressure
levels, have discontinued treatment, although going on
with their daily practice. Some of these have done so even
prior to learning how to relax mental activity. Their fallacy
evidently is wishful thinking, a superconfidence in their
health, which for obvious reasons the doctor does not wish
to shake, even though he may not share it. A more intelligent, if cautious, attitude on the patient's part would be to
follow through on the doctor's instructions, especially after
the merit of those instructions has been proved by the
relief of symptoms.

If you suffer from high blood pressure, you are advised

to consult your physician. When he advises you to relax, as physicians generally do, you are to follow directions as given in Chapters 13 and 14.

Practice especially relaxing the abdominal muscles, for pulling these in raises pressure markedly, in some persons at least. Remember that our evidence suggests that high blood pressure is in part the result of overintense living—nerve and muscle overactivity—and the best remedy that we know to date for this is cultivating relaxation. Do not be dismayed even if your arteries are hardened and your kidneys and heart diseased. If you have an inferior tire on your motorcar, the sensible thing is to use it carefully, avoiding rough roads and glass, to prolong its life. If your organs have ill withstood the wear and tear of life, begin now to conserve them as much as you can by cultivating habits of relaxation.

25

How to Save Your Heart

Our hearts endure much and complain little. They deserve more of us than they receive. When after many years of faithful service, they fail before their time, we ourselves are generally to blame.

From time to time even the finest Swiss watches need to be cleaned and oiled. If this and other needed attention is withheld, they become fast, slow or irregular and sooner or later they stop altogether. But our own uncomplaining hearts demand no such intervention; year in and year out they beat some seventy times per minute or thereabouts with never a squeak about the monotony and repetition. They even change their rate and force to accommodate our needs—and no watch ever does this. When we exercise, they beat faster and harder, and when we rest they relax to permit us to remain quiet.

Unappreciated for their merits, our hearts are sometimes driven by various forms of overuse and abuse until they give signals of distress. Much like the horse, man's friend which can be driven past endurance without overt complaint, our hearts generally make little clamor. Intent in our pursuit of the dollar or whatever else may be our daily interest, we often are heedless of their gentle complaints.

Many is the time when even the *healthy* heart signals to us, "Please, stop!" To be able to note the signal, we must of course give sufficient attention and we must understand a little of the code. Signals include mild pains in the region of the heart, the left shoulder and the left arm. They include also what the patient calls "pounding" and the doctor calls "palpitation". They include skipped beats and other irregularities. They include general body fatigue when severe and protracted.

Pain in the region of the heart, passing to the left shoulder and left arm is known as "angina". Many doctors regard angina as a pain signal which occurs only in diseased hearts. However, my point is that in a mild form angina can occur and often does occur in healthy hearts when subjected to abuse. Asked about such pains, doctors generally belittle them if their patients are healthy. Instead, we all would do well, I believe, to realize that healthy hearts can issue mild complaints worthy of attention. We would do well to recall the adage, "A stitch in time saves nine!"

If people were taught to give more observance to such signals, I believe that many hearts would be saved for longer years of toil. But aside from the weakness of the signals given by the healthy heart when abused, there is quite another difficulty. Even the many heart associations organized for the purpose of public education as a rule give little heed to taking care of the healthy heart. Generally speaking, doctors tend to deride those who give their own health much attention.

Historically there has been much good reason for this. Patients who bear their own health constantly in mind are familiarly known as "neuros" or "hypochondriacs". Their complaints often are out of all proportion to the organic maladies which their doctors can discover.

What has been overlooked, I believe, is the golden mean between overattention and underattention to body and mind. Overattention leads to hypochondria, which is bad; but underattention leads to neglect, which can be worse. In their zeal against hypochondria, doctors have unwittingly encouraged underattention to matters of health not alone in their patients but also in themselves.

So far I have spoken only of healthy hearts and how heedless we often are of their welfare. Among the causes of our neglect, I have mentioned the weakness of the signals of distress offered by our hearts as long as they remain healthy, but also I have been obliged to find fault with current medical teachings insofar as their very contempt for hypochondria offers little encouragement to people to give adequate attention and study to understand how to keep their hearts healthy.

All the more is there need of care of the heart if the blood pressure is high. The pump then has a much heavier job. In early states of hypertension, when the pressure is high only at times, fluctuating at various levels, the heart has ample time for full recovery between the spells of high pressure. At later stages, when the systolic pressure is elevated most or all of the time, there is less rest for the heart. When the diastolic pressure becomes constantly increased, equivalent, for example, to the pressure of a column of one hundred millimeters of mercury or over, there is no single stroke but which demands much more of the heart than is normally required.

Often I am appalled to think of the load which the heart then must carry constantly. Nevertheless, many people live on so, exerting themselves daily in their work and in their play with no thought of their hearts' labors. Their doctors are likely to warn them not to carry luggage or engage in vigorous exercise, lest too much be demanded of their already overburdened organs. Even so, many go on their merry way, living in the world which they wishfully create, where hearts go on forever.

There can come a time when that portion of the heart which pumps the blood to most of the bodily system—the left ventricle—shows signs of overwork. Doctors can recognize these signs in enlargement of the left ventricle as seen in the X-ray and in prolongation of those lines in the electrocardiogram which denote the action of this ventricle. Then in a technical sense they speak of "heart strain".

Heart strain tends in the long run to be fatiguing, whereupon more effort is required for work or for exercise. Contrariwise, work or exercise, if carried too far in persons with heart strain, augments the tendencies toward heart strain. Crudely, we can diagram this vicious circle as follows:

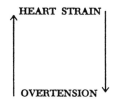

HEART STRAIN

OVERTENSION

Alas! there are limits to the endurance of all hearts. The

final stage of failure which comes to most diseased hearts is probably due to fatigue! I know that you will be surprised to read this, as will many doctors who may chance to scan these pages; but this time I am not responsible for the novelty, if any, of what I have said. Investigators who have tried to find the causes of failure in diseased hearts have searched in vain for structural deficiencies sufficient to explain why the ticking stopped.

In his book *Heart Failure*, Doctor Arthur M. Fishberg relates how investigators have examined diseased hearts post mortem to discover why they stopped beating. No change in their structure different from what clearly had existed for years previously was generally found to explain the cause of death. For this reason it seems most probable that failure in diseased hearts often is due to fatigue of the heart muscle.

If these conclusions are sound, more people die than has been realized from one common cause: fatigue!

Accordingly, we need to arrest the progress of essential hypertension by all means at our disposal before it leads too far along the road to heart strain and extreme heart fatigue.

Good circulation in the heart itself is necessary to avoid heart fatigue. The blood vessels which nourish the muscles in the heart itself are commonly called the "coronary vessels". We know that when these vessels become overtense or spastic, the heart muscle suffers. This is the earlier stage, we believe, of coronary heart disease. Later these vessels may lose their elasticity, becoming hardened. Then the heart becomes less able to meet daily efforts, as in digesting large meals, climbing stairs or walking against a brisk wind. When, because of spasticity or hardening, the coronary vessels fail to have a blood supply adequate for increased exertion of the heart muscle so that it can pump sufficiently to meet the demands resulting from the variable efforts which people often make, the heart fails to get enough oxygen. Gasping for air, so to speak, it cries out in pain. This is what we call angina.

Insufficiency of the coronary vessels thus can occur in an advanced stage of high blood pressure disease, as a sort of development or complication in its progress. In addition, coronary heart disease occurs more or less as a malady in its own right, when high blood pressure often is present, but sometimes is absent.

Unfortunately there are instances when we have no sure means of deciding whether or not coronary disease is present. Electrocardiograms, which are most essential in estimating the location and progress of the disease, sometimes fail us. In a considerable proporton of conditions of coronary heart disease, perhaps about twenty-five per cent, the electrical records do not differ from those secured from hearts known to be healthy. Accordingly in a patient under suspicion, a so-called normal electrocardiogram should not in all cases be taken by the doctor as warranting the reassurance, "Your heart is normal. Go home and forget it!"

We doctors need to remember this and other warnings at times. We are too prone to forget ourselves in our work, prone to believe that the other fellow will get into trouble, not us. Wishful thinking, however, cannot counteract the strains involved in taking one patient's history after another, examining this organ and now that, standing over the operating table, jumping into the car to drive rapidly to deliver the baby and the million and one other duties of the medical day and night.

Mental and emotional strain are potent factors in causing coronary thrombosis, according to Professor John A. Ryle of England. "It is now apparent," he states, "that we shall make small progress with our etiological inquiries while we continue to confine our researches to individual studies in the ward, the consulting-room, the home, and the dead-house. This is a disease of prevalence, a community disease, with particular age and sex associations and a rising national incidence which must surely be related to social changes and to occupational or habitual factors. What, in fact, are the most striking changes in the conduct and conditions of our lives accompanying the steady increase in the disease? The amount of mental work and of mental and emotional stimulation now possible in the course of a single day is something far in excess of anything experienced by our ancestors. The time has come to accept the fact that the pace and pressure of life and their physiological consequences for neuromuscular systems are no longer things to be ignored, as malnutrition in relation to other sickness and mortality was ignored until a few decades ago."

Continuing, Professor Ryle finds in his studies of conditions in England that the male death rate for professional classes from angina is nearly three and a half times that for the working classes. This seems to him to indicate that the conditions of life and work must play an essential role. In fact, he finds among male physicians and surgeons more than three and a half times as many deaths from this disease than among all males in England between the ages of twenty and sixty-five.

Adding to the facts which he secures from the Registrar-General's tables, Professor Ryle further quotes from his own extensive medical experience. Significantly he concludes, "Where modern 'psychosomatic' theory has tended to stress the importance of emotional conflict and repression (which largely reflect temperament), social statistics and clinical histories make a stronger case for such factors as mental overactivity or strain and the day-to-day cares of sustained responsibility, which largely reflect types of employment."

Another Englishman, Sir Henry H. Bashford, agrees that the incidence of coronary disease is some three and a half times greater among professional men, adding that observations made in the Post Office a few years ago fully accord with this; but he disagrees that the amount of mental work and emotional stimulation now possible in the course of a single day is something far in excess of anything experienced by our ancestors, and he doubts that these excesses explain the increased occurrence of this type of heart disease.

As stated in Chapter 1, we can agree with this critic that previous generations doubtless had much to make them nervous. However, we would distinguish, as he does not, between sources of emotional excitement, which doubtless have been many since the days of Adam, and the pace of life due to modern inventions and developments. It is not necessary to go back many years to study the cultures of less developed societies which can be found on earth today—for example, the Mexican Indians apart from large cities. No such pace exists among them as can be noted among the inhabitants of New York and other large North American cities. Furthermore, in America at least, those whose experience extends back into the end of the last century can bear ample witness in their memory of the increased pace and pressure of the present day.

Support for the view of Professor Ryle was found by another English physician, Dr. Donough O'Brien, upon examining the obituary columns of the *Journal of the American Medical Association* from September to November, 1944. In one thousand consecutive notices where the cause was given—and very rarely it was not—twenty-two per cent of the deaths were ascribed to coronary thrombosis. This is not far from twice the number of deaths from this disease in the average population of similar age. These figures suggest that the severe tension of medical practice takes its toll from the heart.

This was not all that Dr. O'Brien's figures revealed. From the same list of one thousand notices he selected those whose worldly fame resulted in an extended obituary notice. Only seven per cent received attention to the extent of fifteen lines or over. Of these, forty-one per cent died of coronary disease—approximately double the number among their less conspicuous colleagues.

Assuming that these figures are fairly representative for American physicians, they suggest that the added effort required to bring fame was the cause, or at least a considerable part of the cause, of the increased incidence of coronary disease in those who achieved relative distinction. Such evidence supports the view that in physicians coronary heart disease to an appreciable extent results from efforts to get ahead.

Once the symptoms of coronary disease make themselves felt in any individual, the result inevitably is to increase his tendency to be overtense. The very knowledge that this malady afflicts his heart cannot but add to the nervous strains from which he suffers. We can depict something of these mutual influences in another diagram of a vicious circle:

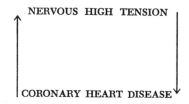

NERVOUS HIGH TENSION

CORONARY HEART DISEASE

Where there is a tendency in the direction of coronary disease, what can be done to break into this vicious circle representing the continuing influences toward breakdown? Most doctors will agree that the avoidance of overeffort and emotional strain is of the utmost importance. Daily rests, along with such activities and mild exercise as may seem permissible in the individual case, are recommended. Avoidance of long working hours, of overeating and of overdrinking, often also of smoking, is generally stressed. My thesis is that, in addition, much can be accomplished through *cultivated* habits of relaxation.

Whether coronary disease can be prevented and lives lengthened by such hygienic measures cannot easily be put to proof. Adequate studies with careful controls would require the passing of decades before conclusions could be regarded as sound. Even then, statistics based upon such studies might be subject to numerous objections from a strictly scientific viewpoint. Accordingly, we cannot soon expect to have a scientific basis for any belief that life can be thus prolonged.

However, it seems only reasonable to assume that if overeffort favors the development of coronary disease leading to death, the counteraction of such overeffort through cultivated relaxation must tend to arrest the development and progress of the disease. Aside from possible prolongation of life, resulting from preventative measures, there remains to be considered the comfort and the efficiency of patients with coronary heart disease. If their ability to carry on their daily work and their capacity to enjoy their leisure can be furthered by relaxation methods, this is no small achievement in itself. If the pain in early coronary disease appears to diminish as the patient becomes progressively less tense, he at any rate appreciates the improvement. To say the least, then, these are the reasonable aims of relaxation treatment, and in some patients I have seen them accomplished.

I have tried to be brief in this chapter, only touching upon some of the important questions raised, and now I must close with a brief summary of advice: Whether healthy or threatened or afflicted with coronary heart disease, if your doctor advises that you are too tense, follow the instructions set forth in Chapters 13 and 14. Perform one tension per day, not as an exercise, for no exercise will teach you to relax, but only as a means of learning to distinguish when and where you are overtense. Remember that once you become able to recognize tension in a part, you are better prepared to relax it. Do not try to complete the tasks assigned in a week or a month, as you will be inclined to do, if and since you are an impatient person. Take your time about it and see what you can do to change your habits.

Don't wear out your heart! If it is healthy or if it is diseased, give it a better chance by *learning to relax*.

Publications by Dr. Jacobson

1910 "Inhibition," doctoral thesis, Harvard University, 1910.

1911 On Meaning and Understanding, *Am. J. Psychol.*, 22: 553–577, October, 1911.

1911 Experiments on the Inhibition of Sensations, *Psychol. Rev.*, 18: 24–53, January, 1911.

1912 Further Experiments on the Inhibition of Sensations, *Am. J. Psychol.*, 23: 345–369, July, 1912.

1917 The Reduction of Gastric Acidity, *J. AMA*, 69: 1767–1768.

1920 Use of Relaxation in Hypertensive States, *N.Y. Med. J.*, Mar 6, 1920.

1920 Reduction of Nervous Irritability and Excitement by Progressive Relaxation, *Trans. Sec. Nervous & Mental Diseases, AMA*, 1920.

1921 Treatment of Nervous Irritability and Excitement, *Illinois Med. J.*, March, 1921.

1921 The Use of Experimental Psychology in the Practice of Medicine, *J. AMA*, 77: 342–347.

1924 The Technic of Progressive Relaxation, *J. Nervous & Mental Disease*, 60 (6): 568–578, December, 1924.

1925 Progressive Relaxation, *Am. J. Psychol.*, 36: 73–87, January, 1925.

1925 Voluntary Relaxation of the Esophagus, *Am. J. Physiol.*, 72 (3): 387–394, May, 1925.

1925 Jacobson, E., and A. J. Carlson: The Influence of Relaxation upon the Knee-jerk, *Am. J. Physiol.*, 73 (2): 324–328, July, 1925.

1926 Response to a Sudden Unexpected Stimulus, *J. Exp. Psychol.*, 9 (1): 19–25, February, 1926.

1927 Spastic Esophagus and Mucous Colitis, *Arch. Internal Med.*, 39: 433–435, March, 1927.

1927 Action Currents from Muscular Contractions during Conscious Processes, *Science*, 66 (1713): 403, Oct. 28, 1927.

1928 Quantitative Recording of the Knee-jerk by Angular Measurement, *Am. J. Physiol.*, 86 (1): 15–19, August, 1928.

1928 Newer Studies of Relaxation and Sleep, *Univ. Chicago Mag.*, 21 (1): 22–25, November, 1928.

1928 Differential Relaxation during Reading, Writing and Other Activities as Tested by the Knee-jerk, *Am. J. Physiol.*, 86 (3): 675–693, October, 1928.

1929 *Progressive Relaxation*, University of Chicago Press, Chicago, May, 1929.

1930 Electrical Measurements of Neuromuscular States during Mental Activities

1. Imagination of Movement Involving Skeletal Muscle, *Am. J. Physiol.*, 91 (2): 567–608, January, 1930.

1930 2. Imagination and Recollection of Various Muscular Acts, *Am. J. Physiol.*, 94 (1): 22–34, July, 1930.

1930 3. Visual Imagination and Recollection, *Am. J. Physiol.*, 95 (3): 694–702, December, 1930.

1930 4. Evidence of Contraction of Specific Muscles during Imagination, *Am. J. Physiol.*, 95 (3): 703–712, December, 1930.

1931 5. Variation of Specific Muscles Contracting during Imagination, *Am. J. Physiol.*, 96 (1): 115–121, January, 1931.

1931 6. A Note on Mental Activities concerning an Amputated Limb, *Am. J. Physiol.*, 96 (1): 122–125, January, 1931.

1931 7. Imagination, Recollection and Abstract Thinking Involving the Speech Musculature, *Am. J. Physiol.*, 97 (1): 200–209, April, 1931.

1932 Electrophysiology of Mental Activities, *Am. J. Psychol.*, 44: 677–694, October, 1932.

1933 Measurement of the Action-potentials in the Peripheral Nerves of Man without Anesthetic, *Proc. Soc. Exp. Biol. & Med.*, 30: 713–715, 1933.

1934 Electrical Measurement of Activities in Nerve and Muscle, from *The Problem of Mental Disorder*, pp. 133–145, McGraw-Hill Book Company, Inc., New York, 1934.

1934 Electrical Measurements concerning Muscular Contraction (Tonus) and the Cultivation of Relaxation in Man, Studies on Arm Flexors, *Am. J. Physiol.*, 107 (1): 230–248, January, 1934.

1934 Electrical Measurements concerning Muscular Contraction (Tonus) and the Cultivation of Relaxation in Man—Relaxation-times of Individuals, *Am. J. Physiol.*, 108 (3) 573–580, June, 1934.

1936 The Course of Relaxation in Muscles of Athletes, *Am. J. Psychol.*, 48: 98–108, January, 1936.

1938 *You Can Sleep Well*, McGraw-Hill Book Company, Inc., New York, 1938.

1938 *Progressive Relaxation*, rev. ed., University of Chicago Press, Chicago, 1938.

1939 The Neurovoltmeter, *Am. J. Psychol.*, 52: 620–624, 1939.

1939 1. Variation of Blood Pressure with Skeletal Muscle Tension and Relaxation, *Ann. Internal Med.*, 12 (8): 1194–1212, February, 1939.

1939 Variations in Blood Pressure with Skeletal Muscle Tension (Action-potentials) in Man.
2. The Influence of Brief Voluntary Contractions, *Am. J. Physiol.*, 126 (3): 546–547, July, 1939.

1940 Variation of Blood Pressure with Skeletal Muscle Tension and Relaxation.
3. The Heart Beat, *Ann. Internal Med.*, 13 (9): 1619–1625, March, 1940.

1940 4. Variation of Blood Pressure with Brief Voluntary Muscular Contractions, *J. Lab. & Clin. Med.*, 25 (10): 1029–1037, July, 1940.

1940 Cultivated Relaxation in "Essential" Hypertension, *Arch. Phys. Therapy*, 21: 645–654, November, 1940.

1940 The Direct Measurement of Nervous and Muscular States with the Integrating Neurovoltmeter (Action-potential Integrator), *Am. J. Psychiat.*, 97 (3): 513–523, November, 1940.

1940 An Integrating Voltmeter for the Study of Nerve and Muscle Potentials, *Rev. Sci. Instr.*, 11(12): 415–418, December, 1940.

1940 *The Principles and Practise of Physical Therapy,* rev. ed., vol. 1, chap. 12, vol. 3, chap. 18, W. F. Prior Co., Hagerstown, 1940.

1940 Jacobson, E., J. E. Lackner, and M. B. Sinykin: Activity of the Human Non-pregnant Uterus, *Am. J. Psychol.,* 53 (3): 407–417, July, 1940.

1941 Recording Action-potentials without Photography, *Am. J. Psychol.,* 54: 266–269, April, 1941.

1941 The Physiological Conception and Treatment of Certain Common "Psychoneuroses," *Am. J. Psychiat.,* 98 (2): 219–226, September, 1941.

1942 The Effect of Daily Rest without Training to Relax on Muscular Tonus, *Am. J. Psychol.,* 55: 248–254, April, 1942.

1942 Jacobson, E., and F. L. Kraft: Contraction Potentials (Right Quadriceps Femoris) in Man during Reading, *Am. J. Physiol.,* 137 (1): 1–5, August, 1942.

1943 Innervation and "Tonus" of Striated Muscle in Man, *J. Nervous & Mental Disease,* 97 (2): 197–203, February, 1943.

1943 Cultivated Relaxation for the Elimination of "Nervous Breakdowns," *Arch. Phys. Therapy,* 24: 133–143, 176, March, 1943.

1943 "Tonus" in Striated Muscle, *Am. J. Psychol.,* 56: 433–437, July, 1943.

1943 Rest: Physical and Mental, *Illinois Med. J.,* 84:2, August, 1943.

1943 Muscular Tension and the Smoking of Cigarettes, *Am. J. Psychol.,* 56: 559–574, October, 1943.

1943 The Cultivation of Physiological Relaxation, *Am. Internal Med.,* 19 (6): 965–972, December, 1943.

1944 Direct Measurements of the Effects of Bromides, Sodium Amytal and of Caffeine in Man, *Ann. Internal Med.*, 21 (3): 455–468, September, 1944.

1946 Electrical Measurements of Mental Activities in Man, *Trans. N.Y. Acad. Sci.*, (2) (8): 272–273, June, 1946.

1947 The Influence of Relaxation upon the Blood Pressure in "Essential Hypertension," *Fed. Proc.*, 6 (1): March, 1947.

1948 Theory of Essential Hypertension in Man, *Trans. N.Y. Acad. Sci.*, (2) 11 (2): 49–50, December, 1948.

1950 Supplement to Rest: Physical and Mental, *Med. Phys.*, vol. 2, 1950.

1952 Specialized Electromyography in Supplement to Clinical Observations during Hyperkinetic States in Man ("Functional Nervous Conditions"), *Fed. Proc.*, 11 (1): March, 1952.

1953 Principles Underlying Coronary Heart Disease (Considerations for a Working Hypothesis), *Cardiologia*, 26: 83, 1955, read before the Am. Assoc. Advance. Sci., Boston, December, 1953.

1955 Neuromuscular Controls in Man: Methods of Self-Direction in Health and in Disease, *Am. J. Psychol.*, 68: 549–561, December, 1955.

1958 Physiological Psychiatry. Basis and Working Principles for a Science of Psychiatry.

1958 How to Relax and Have a Baby. (Completed)

Index

Norephedrine, 224
Normal health, determination of, 64
Norway rats, hypertension experiments on, 220
Nose, examination of, 59

O'Brien, Donough, on coronary thrombosis, 244
Office workers, tension among, 3–4
Old persons and relaxation treatment, 147
Osler, William, on rest, 77
Overactive nerves, 62–69
   causes of, 64–68
   measurement of, 64, 65
   methods for quieting of, 74–83
Overeating and heart trouble, 245
Oxygen, effect of, on blood pressure, 223

Pain, diminished by relaxation, 152
   effect of, on nerves, 66–68
   on sleep, 198–199
Palpitation, 56, 92, 237
Patent medicines, waning popularity of, 58
Pathological conditions affecting nerves, 65–68
Pathological fears, 47, 174
Pavlov, and dog's stomach, 203
   on habit formation, 170
Pearl Harbor, attack on, 7–8
Penicillin, 217
Peptic ulcers, 39–40, 214, 229
Personality, breath-control measures injurious to, 114–115
Philosophy, value of, 80
Phobias, definition of, 174
Physical education, importance of relaxation in, 147
Physical examination, description of, 51–61

Physical examination, importance of, 93
Physicians, heart disease among, 242–245
   inability of, to help tense persons, 54
   relaxation treatment by, 136–137, 140–147
Piéron, Henri, sleep theory of, 191
Pillow in relaxation treatment, 99, 131
Pills, effect of, 57, 163
Piper, H., muscle research by, 154
Pituitary gland and tension, 56
Poison, effect of, on nerves, 66
Poisoning, ptomaine, 10, 67
Posture in sitting position, 134
Practice in relaxation, importance of, 94, 98–99
Primary activities, 137–138
Progressive relaxation, definition of, 87, 97
Progressive Relaxation, 39, 85, 166, 207, 210
Proprioceptive sensations during sleep, 191
Proteins, effect of, on nerves, 10, 79
Pseudoreligious cults, 57, 143, 144
Psychiatric disorders, 6, 62
Psychiatry, and treatment of nervousness, 33, 80
   use of tranquilizers in, 70–71
Psychoanalysis in treatment of nervous disorders, 80
Psychopathic hospitals before World War I, 160
Ptomaine poisoning, 10, 67
Pulse during relaxation and under tension, 88, 89

Quiet necessary during relaxation treatments, 88

Rats, hypertension experiments on, 220

Reading, and differential relaxation, 127–128, 135–138
effect of, on sleep, 182

Recreation, failure of, to relax, 2

Reducing diets, 228–229, 232

Reflexes, 60
arousing of, 153–154
during relaxation, 89

Relaxation, of abdomen, 114, 212–213, 235
of arms, 97, 99–112, 131–132, 134, 141–142
and blood pressure, 88, 89, 91, 225–235
of chest, 114, 120–121
for children, 146–147
and conditions of fear, 47–49, 173–175
definition of, 16–17
of diaphragm, 120–121
differential (*see* Differential relaxation)
of digestive tract, 40, 203–215
of eyes, 100, 105, 108, 115–117, 169–170
mental, 118–119
in sitting position, 135–136
and fatigue, 31, 132, 136, 142, 148, 174
and fear, 47–49, 173–175
general, definition of, 84
program for, 122–123
for heart disease, 17–18, 77, 90–91, 246–247
for high blood pressure, 225–235
hobbies and, 77, 79, 225–226
of internal organs, 91–92
local, 94
measurement of, 29–30, 143, 156–157, 164, 174, 231–232

Relaxation, mental, 117–122, 160–171
and nervous disorders, 138, 141, 172–180
for old people, 147
practice in, importance of, 94, 98–99
progressive, definition of, 87, 94
of respiratory organs, 128
routine during, 278
scientific, 35–38, 74, 76–77, 84–96
for Navy Five, 28–31
in sitting position, 125–126, 131–139
and sleep, 31, 89, 125, 187–202
sports and, 77, 78
superintendence of, by physician, 136–137, 140–147
and surgery, 93
tranquilizers for, 70–73, 75
when active, 124–139
when lying down, 97–123

Religion, influence of, 80

Residual tension, 87–89, 109, 232

Respiration (*see* Breathing)

Respiratory organs, relaxation of, 128

Rest, bed, 81–82
failure of, to relax, 85–86
best time for, 81–82
in chair, 81–82
prescribed, 74, 77
(*See also* Daily nap; Relaxation)

Rest-cure, 138

Restless sleep and dreaming, 193–194, 198–199

Restlessness, of children, 4
prevalence of, 172
as sign of tension, 136

Retiring, time of, 82

Rice diet, effect of, on heart, 14
for high blood pressure, 228–229
Richardson, Henry Handel, on
nervousness, 68–69
Rousseau on modern era, 5
Routine during relaxation treatments, 278
Ryle, John A., on coronary thrombosis, 242–244

Salespersons, importance of relaxation for, 130
tension among, 3
Salt-free diet for high blood pressure, 228–229
Scalp, examination of, 58
Scientific relaxation, 35–38, 74, 76–77, 84–96
Navy Five and, 28–31
Secondary activities, 137–138
Sedatives, 57, 75–76, 124, 199, 200, 233
Sedentary activities, relaxation during, 137
Self-control, lack of, 160
under tension, 141
Sensations, and mental activity, 165–171
proprioceptive, during sleep, 191
and tension, 23–25
unconscious, 111
Sex, resultant tensions of, 2
and theories of nervousness, 149
Sexual maldevelopment, 80
Shakespeare, William, 182
Shock and nervous start, 150–153
Shock treatment, 33
Shoulders during relaxation treatment, 115
Siesta, value of, 81
Singing, importance of relaxation in, 128–129, 147
Sinuses, examination of, 60

Sitting position, relaxation in, 125–126, 131–139
Skeletal muscles, contraction of, 72
relaxation of, 84, 91
Skin, examination of, 60
Skin eruptions, tranquilizers as cause of, 71
Sleep, factors tending to disturb, 182–183
and fatigue, 183–184, 191, 192, 198
and mental activity, 117, 122, 183, 188
nature and importance of, 187–195
neurotic attitudes toward, 184
position for, 99–100
program for, 201–202
quest for, 181–186
and relaxation, 31, 89, 125, 187–202
self-prevention of, 184–186
speech and, 196–197
studies on, 187–195
successful methods for, 196–202
and tension, 10, 51–53, 82, 181–202
(*See also* Insomnia)
Sleep motility, 194
Smith, A. B., on spastic colon, 212
Smoking, and heart trouble, 245
and high blood pressure, 230
Snake-root, 70, 76, 224
Spasm, of coronary arteries, 16, 17
of esophagus, 204–209
of visceral muscles, 91
Spastic colon, 89, 92, 209, 211, 212, 224
Spastic digestive tract, 10–11, 61, 224
Spastic esophagus, 89, 204, 208, 209, 224